A TREASURY OF

Latter-Day Saint

Letters

A TREASURY OF

Latter-day Saint Letters

LARRY E. MORRIS

EAGLE
GATE

To my parents,
Eugene and Velma Morris

Visit us at www.deseretbook.com

Library of Congress Cataloging-in-Publication Data

A treasury of Latter-day Saint letters / [edited by] Larry E. Morris.
  p. cm.
 Includes bibliographical references and index.
 ISBN 1-57345-961-5 (hardcover : alk. paper)
 1. Mormons—United States—Correspondence. I. Morris, Larry E., 1951–

BX8693 .T74 2001
289.3'092'2—dc21   2001001307

Printed in the United States of America   18961-6813

10 9   8   7   6   5   4   3   2   1

CONTENTS

—

PART 4: THE WORK OF THE KINGDOM

PART 5: FELLOWSHIP WITH PUBLIC FIGURES

ACKNOWLEDGMENTS

Thanks to my wife, Deborah, and our children, Isaac, Courtney, Justin, and Whitney, for their love and help while I was working on this book. Thanks to those who encouraged me on this project, especially my sister, Lorraine; my brother, Kent; Uncle Luther and Aunt Lorna Morris; and Aunt Gladys Larsen Clarke, who passed away while the book was in progress. Thanks also to a fine staff of editors at Deseret Book, especially Jana Erickson, who guided this project from the start, Jay Parry, and Jennifer Adams.

Part 1

~

"AND THEY SHALL BE ONE FLESH"

HUSBANDS
AND WIVES

"I Have Visited a Grove . . . Almost Every Day"

JOSEPH SMITH TO EMMA HALE SMITH
6 JUNE 1832

In April of 1832, just one week after they had been beaten and tarred and feathered by a mob of forty drunken men, Joseph Smith and Sidney Rigdon traveled from Ohio to visit the Saints in Independence, Missouri. Newel K. Whitney, ordained a bishop a few months earlier, and Jesse Gause, a former Quaker preacher, accompanied them. During a meeting in Jackson County on 26 April, Joseph, Sidney, Newel, Oliver Cowdery, Martin Harris, and others were appointed through revelation to manage the affairs of the poor (see D&C 82:11–14).

The Prophet, Sidney, and Newel returned to Ohio in May, traveling by stagecoach. As they approached New Albany, Indiana, the horses bolted. Joseph leaped from the runaway stage to safety, but Newel caught his foot in the wheel and broke his leg in several places. Sidney proceeded on to Ohio, but Joseph stayed with his injured companion until Newel was able to travel. During the four-week period in which he cared for Newel, Joseph, twenty-six, wrote the following letter to his wife, Emma, twenty-seven, unaware that she was being shuffled from one residence to another.

June 6th, Greenville, Floyd County, Indiana, 1832
Dear Wife,

I would inform you that Brother Martin [Harris] has arrived here [Greenville, Indiana] and brought the pleasing news that our families were well when he left there, which greatly cheered our hearts and revived our spirits. We thank our Heavenly Father for his goodness unto us and all of you.

Martin arrived on Saturday the same week he left Chagrin

[a town in Ohio] having a prosperous time. We are all in good health. Brother Whitney's leg is gaining, and he thinks he shall be able to perform his journey so as to get home about the 20th. My situation is a very unpleasant one although I will endeavor to be contented, the Lord assisting me.

I have visited a grove which is just back of the town almost every day, where I can be secluded from the eyes of any mortal and there give vent to all the feelings of my heart in meditation and prayer. I have called to mind all the past moments of my life and am left to mourn and shed tears of sorrow for my folly in suffering the adversary of my soul to have so much power over me as he has had in times past. But God is merciful and has forgiven my sins, and I rejoice that he sendeth forth the comforter unto as many as believe and humbleth themselves before him.

I was grieved to hear that Hyrum [Smith] had lost his little child.* I think we can in some degree sympathize with him, but we all must be reconciled to our lots and say the will of the Lord be done. Sister [Elizabeth Ann] Whitney wrote a letter to her husband [Newel K.] which was very cheering, and being unwell at that time and filled with much anxiety, it would have been very consoling to me to have received a few lines from you, but as you did not take the trouble, I will try to be contented with my lot, knowing that God is my friend. In him I shall find comfort. I have given my life into his hands. I am prepared to go at his call. I desire to be with Christ. I count not my life dear to me, only to do his will.

I am not pleased to hear that William McLellin has come back and disobeyed the voice of him who is altogether lovely[,]

---

*Mary Smith, the three-year-old daughter of Hyrum and Jerusha Barden Smith, had died a week earlier, on 29 May 1832, in Kirtland.

for a woman.* I am astonished at Sister Emeline [Miller], yet I cannot believe she is not a worthy sister. I hope she will find him true and kind to her but have no reason to expect it. His conduct merits the disapprobation of every true follower of Christ. But this is a painful subject, [and] I hope you will excuse my warmth of feeling in mentioning this subject and also my inability in conveying my ideas in writing.

I am happy to find that you are still in the faith of Christ and at Father Smith's. I hope you will comfort Father and Mother in their trials and Hyrum and Jerusha and the rest of the family. Tell Sophronia I remember her and Calvin in my prayers.[†] My respects to the rest. I should like to see little Julia[‡] and once more take her on my knee and converse with you on all the subjects which concerns us, things I cannot, is not prudent for me to write. I omit all the important things which, could I see you, I could make you acquainted with.

Tell Brother [Frederick G.] Williams that I and Brother Whitney will arrange the business of that farm when we come. Give my respects to all the Brethren, Br. Whitney's family—tell them he is cheerful and patient and a true brother to me. I subscribe myself your husband. The Lord bless you. Peace be with you, so farewell until I return.

---

*William McLellin had been called on a mission in January 1832. He had discontinued his mission in April, however, and married Emeline Miller.

[†]Joseph's older sister Sophronia had married Calvin Stoddard in December 1827. Stoddard earlier had worked as a carpenter for the Smith family and (according to Lucy) had tried to take possession of the house shortly before the Smiths lost the property. Calvin died in 1836, and Sophronia married William McCleary. She died in Nauvoo in 1876.

[‡]Julia Murdock Smith, adopted daughter of Joseph and Emma, and twin sister of Joseph Murdock. Julia lived most of her life in Nauvoo, near Emma. She married Elisha Dixon in 1849, but the couple did not have any children. Julia died of cancer in 1880, just a year and a half after Emma's death.

Joseph Smith Jr.
(Martin [Harris] will come with us.)

Greenville, Indiana
June 6th, 1832
Mrs. Emma Smith
Kirtland, Geauga County
Ohio

—

Not long after, although Newel had been bedridden for an entire month, Joseph prophesied that if they left the next day they would promptly find a ferry to take them across the Ohio River, then a wagon to take them to a landing. These events unfolded just as Joseph stated, and they were soon traveling up the Ohio toward Kirtland.

Shortly after Joseph and Newel's return, Joseph and Emma moved into three rooms above the Whitney store. Emma began taking in boarders, which became her chief means of income for the next four decades. Early in the fall, Joseph and Newel again departed, this time traveling to New York City.

By 1832, Joseph and Emma had been married for five years and had lost three of the children born to them. They had also lost an adopted child. In the spring of 1831, they had adopted twins Joseph and Julia Murdock. Both children were sick with the measles when the mob attacked in March. Baby Joseph was exposed to the cold, possibly complicating his condition, and he died five days later, on 29 March 1832. Emma was left to mourn in solitude because Joseph and the others left for Missouri just three days after the baby's death. When Joseph wrote his letter from Indiana five weeks later, he probably did not know that Emma was pregnant. This child, born on 6 November 1832, was Joseph III. He lived a full life and died in 1914.

"We Shall Be Delivered from Every Snare"

EMMA HALE SMITH TO JOSEPH SMITH
25 APRIL 1837

During the mid-1830s, Joseph Smith and the Saints in Kirtland, Ohio, "were caught up in the spirit of the times and incurred heavy debts in their efforts to build personal as well as community economic strength. . . . The Church undertook such projects as a steam sawmill, a tannery, and a print shop; and the building of the Kirtland Temple provided employment and some commercial activity. But the Saints, like other western settlers, had little liquid capital, and their business enterprises were begun on credit."[1]

A bank that could print and circulate notes offered a method of paying debts. Late in 1836, Church leaders organized the Kirtland Safety Society Bank. Apostle Orson Hyde traveled to Columbus, Ohio, to obtain a charter. When the request for a charter was denied (the fate of virtually all charter requests in Ohio that year), the Church formed a joint-stock company, called it the Kirtland Safety Society Anti-Banking Company, and began issuing currency. The Kirtland economy boomed and then quickly collapsed.

"In February 1837, a writ was sworn against Joseph for illegal banking. Brought to court March 24, he pleaded that the state law which the Kirtland bank was accused of defying had not been in force when the bank was organized, but the decision went against him, and he was fined a thousand dollars plus costs. Later he appealed, but his appeal was never ruled upon."[2] Joseph, thirty-one, was threatened, and he went into hiding shortly before receiving the following letter from Emma, thirty-two.

Dear Husband,
Your letter was welcomed both by friends and foes; we were glad enough to hear that you was well, and our enemies think

7

they have almost found you, by seeing, where the letters were mailed. We are all well as usual except Mother* is not quite as well as common. Our family is small and yet I have a great deal of business to see to. Brother [name not legible] has not moved yet, and he does not know when he will; we have taken possession of all the room we could get. I have got all the money that I have had any chance to, and as many goods as I could [not legible]. I have not got much at Chester, no money at all, there is so many a watching that place that there is no prospect of my getting anything of consequence there.

Brother Knight[†] will tell you better about the business than I can write, as there is but a moment for me to improve. I cannot tell you my feelings when I found I could not see you before you left, yet I expect you can realize them; the children[‡] feel very anxious about you because they don't know where you have gone; I verily feel that if I had no more confidence in God than some I could name, I should be in a sad case indeed, but I still believe that if we humble ourselves and are as faithful as we can be, we shall be delivered from every snare that may be laid for our feet, and our lives and property will be saved and we redeemed from all unrenderable encumbrances.

My time is out, I pray that God will keep you in purity and safety till we all meet again.

---

*Lucy Mack Smith, sixty-one years old and suffering from severe arthritis.

[†]Probably Vinson Knight, a counselor to Bishop Newel K. Whitney. He was living in Kirtland at the time; he was a charter member and owned stock in the Kirtland Safety Society. Newel Knight, no relation, was apparently in Missouri (Cook, *Revelations*, 265, 78).

[‡]By April 1837, Joseph and Emma had three children: Julia, six; Joseph III, four; and Frederick Granger Williams, almost one year old. Hervey Cowdery, son of Warren Cowdery (and nephew to Oliver), had been indentured to Joseph and Emma and was also living with them at the time.

Emma Smith

Kirtland, April 25th
Mr. Joseph Smith Jr.

—

The crisis in Kirtland escalated throughout the rest of 1837: within months the bank notes were worthless. (Ohio was particularly hard hit in a wave of bank failures that swept across the entire nation. Every bank in Ohio except one stopped redeeming notes.[3]) Many Church members spoke out against Joseph, and early in 1838, he and Sidney Rigdon fled Kirtland for Missouri. Internal strife only increased, however, and during 1838 such prominent leaders as Oliver Cowdery, David and John Whitmer, and Apostles William McLellin, Luke and Lyman Johnson, and John Boynton were all excommunicated.

Persecution of the Saints raged in Missouri, and late in 1838 Joseph and several others were imprisoned in Liberty Jail. In February of 1839, with Joseph still in prison, Emma and her children were forced to leave Missouri. They traveled in a group headed by Stephen Markham. The Mississippi River was frozen, and Emma led her small children across the ice. Carrying two-and-a-half-year-old Frederick and eight-month-old Alexander—as well as two heavy bags filled with Joseph's papers—Emma kept Julia, eight, on one side and Joseph, six, on the other. Fearful that the ice would break, the five of them pushed on through the frigid wind toward Illinois. In a letter to Joseph, Emma wrote: "No one but God, knows the reflections of my mind and the feelings of my heart when I left our house and home, and almost all of everything that we possessed excepting our little children, and took my journey out of the State of Missouri, leaving [you] shut up in that lonesome prison. But the reflection is more than human nature ought to bear, and if God does not record our sufferings and avenge our wrongs on them that are guilty, I shall be sadly mistaken."[4]

"We Have One Little Angel in Heaven"

PHOEBE CARTER WOODRUFF TO WILFORD WOODRUFF
18 JULY 1840

In April of 1837, Wilford Woodruff married Phoebe Whitmore Carter. Wilford had been baptized just three years before their marriage, and a month after it, he left on a six-month mission to the Fox Islands. Wilford and Phoebe's first child was born in July of 1838, a daughter named Sarah Emma. In May of 1839, shortly after his ordination as an apostle, Wilford joined his family in Montrose, Iowa, across the Mississippi River from Commerce, Illinois—later renamed Nauvoo. Three months later Wilford left on another mission, this time to England. The couple's second child, Wilford Jr., was born in March of 1840, while Wilford was in England. Several months after that, Wilford received the following letter from Phoebe.

My Dear Wilford, what will be your feelings, when I say that yesterday I was called to witness the departure of our little Sarah Emma from this world. Yes, she is gone. The relentless hand of death has snatched her from my embrace. But Ah! She was too lovely, too kind, and too affectionate to live in this wicked world. When looking on her I have often thought how I should feel to part with her. I thought I could not live without her, especially in the absence of my companion. But she has gone. The Lord hath taken her home to himself for some wise purpose.

It is a trial to me, but the Lord hath stood by me in a wonderful manner. I can see and feel that he has taken her home and will take better care of her than I possibly could, for a little while until I shall go and meet her. Yes Wilford, we have one little angel in heaven, and I think it likely her spirit has visited you before this time.

It is hard living without her. She used to call her poor papa many times in a day. She left a kiss for her papa with me just before she died. She ate her dinner as well as usual Thursday. Was taken about 4 O'clock with a prestness for breath. The elders laid hands upon her and anointed her a number of times, but the next day her spirit took its flight from this to another world without a groan.

Today Wilford and I with quite a number of friends accompanying us came over to Commerce to pay our last respects to our little darling in seeing her decently buried. She had no relative to follow her to the grave or to shed a tear for her but her Ma and little Wilford. I have just been to take a pleasing melancholy walk to Sarah's grave; she lies alone in peace. I can say that the Lord gave and the Lord hath taken away and blessed be the name of the Lord.

Phoebe W. Woodruff

As Wilford noted in his journal, Sarah Emma died on 17 July 1840, three days after her second birthday. However, he did not receive the letter until 26 October. A year later, in the fall of 1841, Wilford returned from England to find both Phoebe and young Wilford sick. Wilford Sr. set to work harvesting hay, and, although he himself soon fell ill, he continued working and preaching to the Saints. He moved the family into a house in Nauvoo, noting on 19 October that he and Phoebe had spent a night under their own roof for the first time since they were married.

Wilford Woodruff, who died in 1898 at age ninety-two, was an amazing journal keeper, with diaries from 1833 to 1898 that comprise more than 7,000 manuscript pages. Wilford's biographer, Matthias F. Cowley, noted that "the frankness of his expressions, his care for details, and his conscientious regard for the truth made him, perhaps, the best chronicler of events in all the history of the Church."[1]

Of Wilford and Phoebe's nine children, five died in infancy, two of them on the trek west in November and December of 1846. Phoebe, frequently separated from Wilford because of his almost continual missions, lived to age seventy-eight and died in Salt Lake City in 1885. "Little Wilford" was the last surviving member of the family when he died in 1921 at age eighty-one.

"I Dream about You Almost Every Night"

DIANTHA FARR CLAYTON TO WILLIAM CLAYTON
16 MARCH 1846

Englishman William Clayton was twenty-three years old when he converted to Mormonism in 1837. Within months he was called to the British Mission presidency. Three years later Clayton and his family emigrated to Nauvoo, where William became a friend and confidant of Joseph Smith. Once William "became acquainted with the Mormon prophet, his awe quickly turned to unwavering personal loyalty."[1]

In 1843, while the practice was still secret, William took his first plural wife. He had three wives and was thirty years old when he proposed to sixteen-year-old Diantha Farr. Diantha's parents agreed, and William and Diantha were married in January of 1845. Diantha continued to live with her parents, however, and was not free to tell others about the marriage. In February of 1846, William was required to go west with the Saints. Diantha, only a month away from delivering her first child, was unable to accompany William and his three other wives, Ruth Moon, Margaret Moon, and Alice Hardman. Diantha wrote the following letter less than three weeks after the others left.

My beloved but absent William,

It rejoiced my heart to hear a word from you, but it would have given me more joy to have had a line from you, but I am thankful for a little—you know, that is the way to get more. To tell you I want to see you is useless yet true; you are constantly in my mind by day, and I dream about you almost every night. As to my health, it is about the same as when you left only a little more so. I often wish you had taken your house along for it looks so lonesome. It seems a long time since I saw you, but how much longer it will be before I can have the privilege of conversing with you face to face it is yet unknown to me. Father is [illegible word] as fast as he can; he wants to get away soon, after conference if possible. Mother sends her best respects to you, and often says how lonesome it seems. Don't you think William will come tonight? I expect it would cheer her heart as well as mine to hear your voice once more. Dear William, as often as you can send, for one line from you would do my heart good. I must draw to a close, for I am in haste. I will try to compose myself as well as I can. I never shall consent to have you leave again.

Farewell, Farewell

Two weeks after writing this letter, Diantha gave birth to a son. (The couple would later name him Moroni.) Two weeks after that, after spending a difficult night on watch, William received word of the birth; he also learned that Diantha would be able to join him. In this rich atmosphere that combined both hardship and joy, William Clayton penned the words to a hymn that would inspire countless Saints, both present and future: "All Is Well," now known as "Come, Come, Ye Saints."

At the end of June, William rode to Mt. Pisgah, Iowa, to meet Diantha and baby Moroni. He wrote in his journal: "Diantha was very glad to see me and burst into tears. My little boy is far beyond all my expectations. He is very fat and well formed and has a noble countenance. They are both well and I feel to thank my heavenly Father for his mercies to them. . . ."[2]

The story has a sorrowful ending. Less than a month after giving birth to her third child, a daughter named Rachel, Diantha Farr Clayton died, on 11 September 1850. She was twenty-one years old. Moroni, the son who brought William such great rejoicing, died in 1864 at the age of eighteen, and Rachel succumbed to childbirth complications at age twenty-one. Only Olive, the second child, survived William Clayton, who died in 1879 at age sixty-five.

"This Separation Is Bitterly Hard"

CAMILLA EYRING KIMBALL TO SPENCER W. KIMBALL
14 NOVEMBER 1933

In 1933, Spencer and Camilla Kimball had been married for almost six-teen years and were living in Safford, Arizona. On Tuesday 5 September, shortly before his third birthday, their son Eddie "came inside from playing and complained of a sore throat. He vomited and his temperature shot up. By Thursday he had difficulty in standing. On Saturday, when he stood up from his chair, his leg collapsed under him and he fell to the floor. As he slept his muscles twitched. Fully alarmed, Camilla rushed him to a doctor, who diag-nosed the problem as arthritis or possibly diphtheria."[1]

Within days, however, Spencer and Camilla discovered that Eddie's symptoms matched those of a neighborhood girl who had had polio. Leaving their three other children—Spencer LeVan, fifteen; Olive Beth, eleven; and Andrew, six—at home, they left the next morning for an orthopedic hospital in Los Angeles, driving the entire day and night. A doctor confirmed that Eddie indeed had polio and ordered three days of isolation. It was Eddie's third birthday.

Spencer had to return to Safford after ten days, but Camilla stayed in California with Eddie for another two and a half months. They were thus separated on their anniversary—16 November. They wrote the following letters to each other:

Nov. 14, 1933

My beloved Husband,

The day you receive this note will mark the sixteenth anniversary [of] our wedding. Our first separation on that day.

I wanted to tell you again as I perhaps do too often how much I love and appreciate you. Every year increases my love and respect. This separation is bitterly hard but it has made me realize more than ever before how much I have to be thankful for. The fact that never once in the time of our acquaintance have I found cause to doubt or mistrust is I consider one of the foundation stones upon which real happiness and contentment in marriage is built. The attraction of sex and other things of course combine to make the perfect union but without confidence there can be nothing lasting.

I feel that our trouble has drawn us even closer together in spirit though temporarily we are separated.

My constant prayer is that God will preserve the unity of our family and that we may soon all be together again. The joy of that day will be immeasurable.

How I long for you and the strength received from your beautiful character. There is no other so fine and so true.

> Your devoted wife,
> Camilla

"You Are the Finest Wife in the World"

⌒

Tuesday morning

My darling wife

. . . Sixteen years is a long time for a girl to put up with one man and especially such a poor excuse as I am so I honor you on this anniversary. It has been [an] extremely happy sixteen years. We have had our ups and downs, our disappointments and our surprises, our joys and our sorrows, and it has been a wonderful period. I want you to know that I love and appreciate you. You are the finest wife in the world and I am not unmindful of it even though I do seem thoughtless at times. . . .

Affectionately,

Spencer

⌒

Eddie recovered from the polio attack to some extent. All of "Camilla's work and prayer, and a series of half a dozen operations between 1936 and 1940, left Eddie still substantially handicapped. Finally he could walk without braces or crutches, but awkwardly. Though this was not the complete recovery the family had hoped for, he had been small enough when polio struck that he grew up with the condition and felt little self-pity."[2]

Spencer and Camilla Kimball had just celebrated their sixty-eighth anniversary when President Kimball died in December of 1985 at age ninety. Camilla died two years later at age ninety-two. Edward L. Kimball ("Eddie") graduated from the University of Utah Law School and is now a retired professor of law at the J. Reuben Clark Law School at Brigham Young University. He coauthored biographies of both his parents and has published several historical articles.

Loving Welfare Service in War-Ravaged Europe

EZRA TAFT BENSON TO FLORA AMUSSEN BENSON
17 SEPTEMBER 1946

In January of 1946, forty-six-year-old Ezra Taft Benson, a member of the Quorum of the Twelve for just over two years, was called by the First Presidency to reopen the missions in Europe and provide welfare to the European Saints. World War II had ended only eight months earlier. Frederick W. Babbel, who had served in the Swiss-German Mission before the war, accompanied Elder Benson. The first American citizens authorized to travel in all four occupied areas of Germany, Elder Benson and Brother Babbel experienced one miracle after another as they attempted to assist Church members, many of whom had lost their homes and their livelihoods in the war.

Despite endless regulations and red tape, Elder Benson found ways to reach the Saints. In a typical experience, he and Brother Babbel felt inspired to visit Polish territory in East Prussia. However, they were unable to obtain visas at the Polish embassy in London. In Brother Babbel's words, " . . . Elder Benson said quietly but firmly, 'Let me pray about it.'

"Some two or three hours after President Benson had retired to his room to pray, he stood in my doorway and said with a smile on his face, 'Pack your bags. We are leaving for Poland in the morning!'"

The two men flew to Berlin and somehow received permission to travel to Poland, although the Polish Military Mission in Berlin technically lacked such authority. When they arrived in Poland, they drove to the village of Zelbak, hoping to find members of a German branch that had been located there. The village was empty, but they saw a woman hiding behind a large tree.

"Her expression was one of fear as we stopped, but upon learning who we were she greeted us with tears of gratitude and joy. . . .

" . . . Within minutes the cry went from house to house, 'The brethren are here! The brethren are here!' Soon we found ourselves surrounded by about fifty of the happiest people we had ever seen."[1]

Elder Benson refers to this visit to Poland in the following letter to his wife, Flora, forty-five.

—

Tuesday, September 17, 1946

Berlin, Germany

Just a hurried note while waiting for my next appointment here in the Office of Military Government U. S. (OMGUS). I have just been to the finance office, where I was the first person to receive the new currency which goes into effect today with all the military U. S. forces in Germany. For three days everything has been closed for purchases or sales pending the changeover. The introduction of the new currency is an effort to control the black market. This money is different from what the Germans have, so the new money can be used only in military places. Of course, this will not prevent Americans from buying cigarettes, etc., at the army store (PX) and exchanging them secretly for German articles on the black market, but there is a limit to the quantity of cigarettes, candy, etc., that each soldier can purchase.

Well, darling, I'm not going to Poland. The authorities advise against it and the Polish military officials here seem to be against it. In fact, they've told me that I shouldn't have traveled freely in Poland contacting our German Saints as I did before. For some good reason, I did not learn of their strict rules and so proceeded to do the work we needed to do and, after accomplishing our mission, reported to the authorities what we'd done.

When I talk with my good Polish friend here who is head of

the Polish Military Mission, he tells me that the officials in Poland are surprised I traveled about the nation without being stopped—and apparently they are somewhat displeased. But as our Ambassador Murphy said to me yesterday, "Mr. Benson, it's fortunate for you, I suppose, that you were not familiar with all their restrictions or else you would not have been able to contact your people in Poland at all."

So again the Lord has worked things out for us in a most peculiar way, and all is well because most of our people are now out of Poland according to information received since coming into Germany. Our assistance was just in time.

Honey dear, it seems so different on this trip. For one thing the weather is lovely. The surroundings here at U. S. headquarters have been greatly improved, and many of the traces of war have been removed. However, when one goes into other parts of the city, all is destruction and poverty, and one soon has a feeling of sadness and despondency.

Although the condition of the people is somewhat improved, one of the serious matters is that there is as yet no fuel available for the Germans for the winter ahead. In our meeting yesterday with the acting mission presidency, they wrapped themselves in blankets because already the nights and mornings here are cold. Fortunately for the mission home, the brethren followed my suggestion this spring and cut down three huge trees to let in some sunlight for the garden and have cut them all up and have them stored under cover. This will be a great help during the coldest weather. . . .

After traveling more than sixty thousand miles during his ten months in Europe, Elder Benson returned to the United States in December of 1946, three months after writing the above letter. Along with coordinating the delivery of ninety-three railroad carloads of food, clothing, and other supplies, he had spoken to many gatherings of Saints and dedicated the land of Finland for the preaching of the gospel.

Ezra and Flora had six children and celebrated their sixty-fifth anniversary in 1991. From 1953 to 1961, Ezra Taft Benson served as Secretary of Agriculture under President Dwight D. Eisenhower. Flora died in 1992, at age ninety-one, seven years after Elder Benson became President of the Church. President Benson died in 1994, at age ninety-four.

"The Enduring Love Which Has Grown through the Years"

HUGH B. BROWN TO ZINA CARD BROWN

25 DECEMBER 1962

—

Hugh B. Brown was an eighteen-year-old cowboy in 1902 when he first met Zina Young Card, the thirteen-year-old daughter of Charles O. Card, stake president and founder of Cardston, Alberta, Canada. When Hugh saw the petite Zina give a recitation, he said to his mother, "Some day I am going to marry that girl." His mother replied, "I hope you will."

Hugh returned from his mission to England late in 1906, and a few months later he visited the Cards in Salt Lake City, where they had moved after President Card's death in 1906. Hugh went to the Lion House, where her mother Zina—Zina Presendia Young Card, a daughter of Brigham Young—was working. When he requested young Zina's hand in marriage, the elder Zina replied, "You can't have her. I won't let her go back to Canada. I've had enough heartache and heartbreak in that country myself."

"All I ask of you, Aunt Zina," said Hugh, "is to be neutral in the case and let me fight my own battles." This she agreed to do. A short time later, however, she consulted Hugh's former mission president, Apostle Heber J. Grant. "I have seven daughters," he said. "Hugh Brown can choose any one of them. That's what I think of Hugh Brown."[1]

Though she was engaged to someone else when Hugh first proposed, young Zina eventually agreed to marry Hugh. Almost fifty-five years later, on Christmas day 1962, Zina, seventy-four, received a diamond and the following note from Hugh, seventy-nine.

—

Sweetheart:

Fifty-five years ago I was looking forward to June when you would become my bride. I bought the best gem my meager means would permit.

Since then you have given me eight of the most precious jewels of earth or heaven.

Only a diamond can symbolize the enduring love which has grown through the years.

God bless and spare you to me and us that our love may continue to grow throughout eternity.

Your own forever,

Hugh

———

In his memoirs, Hugh B. Brown wrote, " . . . Zina and I were married in the Salt Lake Temple by President Joseph F. Smith [then President of the Church]. No man ever had a truer wife, a better companion, nor was there ever a better mother in the world than my wife, Zina Young Card Brown."[2]

Hugh and Zina had been married for sixty-six years when Zina died in December of 1974.

Hugh followed her in death one year later. They had six daughters and two sons. Their older son, Hugh Card Brown, joined the Royal Air Force in World War II and was lost over the North Sea in March of 1942. The other children all lived to see Hugh Sr.'s ninetieth birthday celebration in 1973.

Part 2

—

"BORN OF GOODLY PARENTS"

BELOVED
FAMILIES

"My Husband Was Taken from Me by an Armed Force"

MARY FIELDING SMITH TO JOSEPH FIELDING

JUNE 1839

Born in Bedfordshire, England, in 1801, Mary Fielding immigrated to Toronto, Canada, in 1834, joining her brother Joseph and sister Mercy. In 1836, Apostle Parley P. Pratt arrived in Toronto to preach the gospel. He soon met a turner shop owner and Methodist Church member by the name of John Taylor. In the words of Parley P. Pratt:

"John Taylor accompanied me—this was before he was baptized—we rode on horseback. We called at a Mr. Fielding's, an acquaintance and friend of Mr. Taylor's. This man had two sisters [Mary and Mercy], young ladies, who seeing us coming ran from their house to one of the neighboring houses, lest they should give welcome, or give countenance to 'Mormonism.' Mr. Fielding stayed, and as we entered the house he said he was sorry we had come. . . . [He] said, 'we don't want a new religion contrary to the Bible.' 'Oh!' said I, 'If that is all we shall soon remove your prejudices. Come, call home your sisters, and let's have some supper.' . . .

"The honest man consented. The young ladies came home, got us a good supper, and all went to meeting. The house was crowded; I preached, and the people wished to hear more. The meeting house was opened for further meetings, and in a few days we baptized brother Joseph Fielding and his two amiable and intelligent sisters, for such they proved to be in an eminent degree."[1]

The Fieldings soon joined the Saints in Kirtland, Ohio, and met the Prophet Joseph Smith and his brother Hyrum. On 13 October 1837, Hyrum's first wife, Jerusha Barden Smith, died at age thirty-two. Joseph urged Hyrum, now a widower with five young children (ranging in age from two weeks to ten years), to remarry quickly. Hyrum and Mary Fielding were married on Christmas Eve, 24 December 1837, and their son, Joseph F. Smith, was born in Far West, Missouri, on 13 November 1838. Two weeks later Hyrum, Joseph, and four others* were imprisoned in Liberty Jail, where they remained until 6 April 1839. Mary, thirty-seven, wrote the following letter to her brother two months after their release. Joseph Fielding, who had been called as one of the first seven missionaries to England,† was then forty-two.

Commerce,‡ Illinois, North America

June, 1839

My very dear Brother,—

As the elders are expecting shortly to take their leave of us again to preach the Gospel in my native land, I feel as though I would not let the opportunity of writing you pass by unimproved. I believe it will give you pleasure to hear from us by our own hand; notwithstanding you will see the brethren face to face, and have an opportunity of hearing all particulars respecting us and our families, from their mouths.

As it respects myself, it is now so long since I wrote to you, and so many important things have transpired, and so great have been my afflictions, &c., that I know not where to begin; but I can say, hitherto has the Lord preserved me, and I am still living to praise Him, as I do this day. I have, to be sure, been called to drink deep of the bitter cup; but you know, my beloved brother, this makes the sweet the sweeter. I feel at this moment, while reflecting on the events of the past seven months, so full of

---

*Sidney Rigdon, Lyman Wight, Alexander McRae, and Caleb Baldwin.

†Heber C. Kimball and Orson Hyde of the Quorum of the Twelve and Willard Richards, Joseph Fielding, John Goodson, Isaac Russell, and John Snider arrived in England on 19 July 1837.

‡Later Nauvoo.

matter, that I am ready to wish I could convey myself into your presence for a short time, so that I might communicate verbally more than I can possibly do by the pen.

You have, I suppose, heard of the imprisonment of my dear husband, with his brother, Joseph, Elder Rigdon, and others, who were kept from us nearly six months; and I suppose no one felt the painful effects of their confinement more than myself. I was left in a way that called for the exercise of all the courage and grace I possessed. My husband was taken from me by an armed force, at a time when I needed, in a particular manner, the kindest care and attention of such a friend, instead of which, the care of a large family was suddenly and unexpectedly left upon myself and, in a few days after, my dear Little Joseph F. was added to the number. Shortly after his birth I took a severe cold, which brought on chills and fever; this, together with the anxiety of mind I had to endure, threatened to bring me to the gates of death. I was at least four months entirely unable to take any care either of myself or child; but the Lord was merciful in so ordering things that my dear sister [Mercy] could be with me all the time. Her child was five months old when mine was born; so she had strength given her to nurse them both, so as to have them do well and grow fast.

You will also have heard of our being driven, as a people, from the state,* and from our homes, but you will hear all particulars from the elders, so as to render it not necessary for me to write them; this happened during my sickness, and I had to be removed more than 200 miles, chiefly on my bed. I suffered much on my journey; but in three or four weeks after we got into Illinois, I began to mend, and my health is now as good as ever it

---

*The Saints were driven from Missouri early in 1839.

was. It is now little more than a month since the Lord, in his marvellous power, returned my dear husband, with the rest of the brethren, to their families, in tolerable health. We are now living in Commerce, on the bank of the great Mississippi river. The situation is very pleasant; you would be much pleased to see it. How long we may be permitted to enjoy it I know not; but the Lord knows best what is best for us. I feel but little concerned about where I am, if I can but keep my mind staid upon God; for, you know in this there is perfect peace. I believe the Lord is overruling all things for our good. I suppose our enemies look upon us with astonishment and disappointment.

I greatly desire to see you, and I think you would be pleased to see our little ones; will you pray for us, that we may have grace to train them up in the way they should go, so that they may be a blessing to us and the world. I have a hope that our brothers and sisters will also embrace the fulness of the Gospel, and come into the new and everlasting covenant; I trust that their prejudices will give way to the power of truth. I would gladly have them with us here, even though they might have to endure all kind of tribulation and affliction with us and the rest of the children of God, in these last days, so that they might share in the glories of the celestial kingdom. As to myself, I can truly say, that I would not give up the prospect of the latter-day glory for all that glitters in this world.

O! my dear brother, I must tell you, for your comfort, that my hope is full, and it is a glorious hope; and though I have been left, for near six months, in widowhood, in the time of great affliction, and was called to take joyfully or otherwise the spoiling of almost all our goods, in the absence of my husband, and all unlawfully, just for the Gospel's sake, (for the judge himself declared, that he was kept in prison for no other reason than because he was a friend to his brother,) yet I do not feel the least discouraged; no, though my sister and I are here together in a strange land, we have been enabled to rejoice, in the midst of our privations and persecutions, that we were counted worthy to suffer these things so that we may, with the ancient saints who suffered in like manner inherit the same glorious reward. If it had not been for this hope, I should have sunk before this; but, blessed be the God and Rock of my salvation, here I am, and am perfectly satisfied and happy, having not the smallest desire to go one step backward.

Your last letter to Elder [Heber C.] Kimball gave us great pleasure; we thank you for your expression of kindness, and pray God to bless you according to your desires for us.

The more I see of the dealings of our Heavenly Father with us as a people, the more I am constrained to rejoice that I was ever made acquainted with the everlasting covenant. O may the Lord keep me faithful till my change come! I desire that you would write us, and let us know all particulars that would be interesting to us. Oh, my dear brother, why is it that our friends should stand out against the truth, and look on those that would show it to them as their enemies? The work here is prospering much; several men of respectability and intelligence, who have been acquainted with all our difficulties, are coming into the work.

Sister Mercy will also write to you. My husband joins me in love to you. I remain, my dear brother and sister,* your affectionate sister,

Mary Smith

———

*Joseph had married Hannah Greenwood while in England.

Joseph Fielding remained in England another two years and served as president of the British Mission. He held leadership positions in Winter Quarters and arrived in the Salt Lake Valley in 1848, living there until his death in December of 1863, at age sixty-six.

Hyrum and Mary had their second child, Martha Ann, in May of 1841, three months before they lost seven-year-old Hyrum (Jerusha's fourth child). Hyrum Sr. died three years later at Carthage Jail, and Mary crossed the plains with her sister Mercy and her brother Joseph Fielding and his family. "When in distress, she relied on the Lord to guide [her] to her lost cattle and to heal her oxen. She died in Salt Lake City on 21 September 1852, four years after reaching the valley. Remembered for her refinement, courage, and tenderness, Mary was a 'saint if ever one lived on this troubled earth. She was a heroine in her own right by reason of her greatness of spirit and soul.'"[2]

"You Dwell in My Bosom, in My Heart"

JOHN TAYLOR TO HIS FAMILY

1850

—

At the October conference of 1849, two years after he had arrived in the Salt Lake Valley, Apostle John Taylor was called on a mission to France. He left on the nineteenth of that month. "In the same company were Lorenzo Snow, bound for Italy; Erastus Snow, for Denmark; Franklin D. Richards, for England; besides some eight or ten other Elders for various fields of labor, and a number of brethren for the Eastern States on business."[1] (Elders Lorenzo Snow, Erastus Snow, and Franklin Richards were also members of the Quorum of the Twelve.)

Two days after the group passed Fort Laramie, Wyoming, while they were watering their horses, a band of two hundred well-armed Indians appeared on the crest of a hill and charged at them. The elders hastily prepared for a possible battle but held their fire. Luckily, the chiefs were peaceful, and one of them produced a paper stating that their tribe, the Cheyenne, was friendly to whites. The brethren later visited several of their lodges and were well received.

After spending time in Kanesville, Iowa, the elders continued on to St. Louis, where John Taylor, forty-one, wrote the following letter to his family:

—

My Dear Family:

After a long absence I now sit down to write to you. I have been in this city about three weeks, and stayed in Kanesville about as long. I have been going leisurely along for the purpose of studying French, that I might be the better prepared to enter on my mission on my arrival in France. I have made some progress in the language and hope to be able to speak it on my arrival there. The Saints wherever I go treat me with the greatest kindness and hospitality.

The latter part of our journey over the plains was a cold and dreary one, but the Lord was with us and protected us, and opened out our way before us. The snows fell on our right and left, before and behind, but we never encountered a snow storm until the last day. We arrived safe, however, and all is well.

At Kanesville we were saluted with the firing of guns on our arrival, and the greatest manifestations of rejoicing, and parties, musical entertainments, etc., were gotten up. This has also been the case in St. Louis.* Here the Saints have a magnificent hall and a splendid band and do things up in good style. . . . But these outward tokens of friendship are very little to me, when compared with the heart-felt joy, the kindly feeling, the sympathetic and warm-hearted brotherhood manifested by many of my old friends, hundreds of whom seem anxious in every possible way to promote my happiness, secure my company and have my blessing and friendship. On my arrival both here and in Kanesville the Saints flocked around me like bees; and the greatest trouble I have is that of not being able to fulfill the many engagements that have pressed themselves upon me.

"But," say you, "do you not think of us and home? and do you never think of me, and of me?" This is what I have been wanting to get at for some time, and this long, tedious preface has become wearisome to me—let me tell my feelings if I can. Home! Home! Home! What shall I say? can I tell it? No, a thousand times no! Your forms, your countenances, your bodies and your spirits are all portrayed before me as in living characters. You are with me

---

*In 1850 there were several branches of the Church in St. Louis and close to three thousand members (Roberts, 206).

in my imaginations, thoughts, dreams, feelings; true our bodies are separated, but there you live—you dwell in my bosom, in my heart and affections, and will remain there forever. Our covenants, our hopes, our joys are all eternal and will live when our bodies moulder in the dust. Oceans, seas, mountains, deserts and plains may separate us—but in my heart you dwell.

Do I see an amiable, lovely woman—my feelings are not there, they fly to my home. Do I see a beautiful infant—hear the prattle of lovely innocents, or the symmetry and intelligence of those more advanced in years? My mind flies to my home—there I gaze upon my wives, there I fondle and kiss my children and revel for a time in this mental delight; but I awake from my reverie and find that it is but a dream, and that mountains, deserts and plains separate us! Do I murmur? No! Do you? I hope not—shall I not say for you, No?

I am engaged in my Master's business; I am a minister of Jehovah to proclaim His will to the nations. I go to unlock the door of life to a mighty nation, to publish to millions the principles of life, light and truth, intelligence and salvation, to burst their fetters, liberate the oppressed, reclaim the wandering, correct their views, improve their morals, save them from degradation, ruin and misery, and lead them to light, life, truth and celestial glory. Do not your spirits co-operate with mine? I know they do. Do you not say, "Go, my husband, go, my father; fulfill your mission, and let God and angels protect you and restore you safe to our bosoms?" I know you do. Well, our feelings are reciprocal, I love my family and they love me; but shall that love be so contracted, so narrow, so earthly and sensual as to prevent my doing the will of my Father in heaven? No, say I, and you echo, No. No! our thoughts and feelings soar in another atmosphere. We live for time, and we live for eternity; we love here and we will love forever—

While life or thought or being last,

Or immortality endures!

Our separations here tend to make us more appreciative of each other's society. A few more separations and trials, a few more tears, a few more afflictions, and the victory will be ours! We'll gain the kingdom, possess the crown, inherit eternal glory, associate with the Gods, soar amidst the intelligences of heaven; and with the noble, the great, the intellectual, the virtuous, the amiable, the holy, possess the reward held in reserve for the righteous, and live and love forever. . . . May the spirit of peace be and abide with you forever; and when you bow before the Throne of Grace remember your affectionate husband, father and friend.

On 18 June 1850, Elder Taylor and Curtis E. Boulton arrived in France to work with William Howell, a Welsh member of the Church who had founded the French mission a year earlier.* They were soon joined by John Pack,† who had accompanied John Taylor from Utah.

Not long after arriving in France, Elder Taylor was challenged to a debate by three English ministers. "The debate was to run for three nights, seven to ten, each party having thirty minutes alternately, with three officials of the Church of England as chairmen. The subjects would be, first, Joseph Smith: 'Was he a truthful and honest man, or a blasphemous and daring imposter?'; second, the Book of Mormon: 'Is it . . . a revelation from God . . . [or] stupid

---

*William Howell had organized the first branch in France at Boulogne on 6 April 1850, with six members. This was exactly twenty years after Joseph Smith organized the Church itself with six members (Taylor, 147, n2).

†John Taylor reprimanded Elder Pack several times for publicly discussing plural marriage, which Elder Taylor felt must remain secret (see Taylor, 146–158).

and ignorant farago of nonsense?' and third, 'Yourselves! The pretended facts of your Direct Appointment by God, to preach what you call the Gospel.'"[2] Admission was one-half franc, which was to be donated to the poor after expenses were met. (John Taylor felt that he won the debate, but Elder Boulton was not nearly as confident.)

After almost two years of traveling back and forth between France, Germany, and England—supervising the translation of the Book of Mormon into both French and German; holding conferences; publishing pamphlets; and even witnessing troops storm Paris with the *coup d'etat* of Louis Napoleon—John Taylor left for the United States in March of 1852. He was reunited with his family on 20 August 1852, thirty-four months after he had left.

Counsel to a Missionary Son

JOSEPH F. SMITH TO JOSEPH FIELDING SMITH
20 JUNE 1899

As a young man, Joseph Fielding Smith attended Latter-day Saint College and worked at ZCMI department store. On 26 April 1898, he married Emily Louie Shurtliff; they were both twenty-one. The temple sealing was performed by Joseph's father, Joseph F. Smith, then a counselor in the First Presidency. One year later, at age twenty-two, Joseph Fielding was called on a mission to England. He received the following letter from his father, sixty, shortly after he arrived in England.

June 20, 1899

I am glad to hear that the people of the ship treated you kindly and that you did not see any occasion to find fault with anything except the slow progress of the voyage. As for scoffing unbelievers, it is not worth your while to waste time or the energy of your thought on them. Let your mind turn as it naturally does upon the duties of your mission and calling. Do not stop to trouble yourself about what the world may think of you, or what enemies may say about you. Of one thing be sure, that is, that you are in fellowship with the Almighty, and have a conscience void of offence towards all men. Do not seek to excel men, only seek to do your duty faithfully and well, leaving all the results in the hands of the Lord. It will then be well with you both in time and in eternity. . . .

There is nothing that could give me more joy and satisfaction than the realization which I have that you possess the spirit of the Gospel and have received the testimony of its truth. God bless you forever in this regard, my son, and cause you to develop in mind and to grow in understanding and in the knowledge of His truth until you shall know as you are known and see as you are seen. And withal, I admonish you to use judgment and cultivate patience and humility; be not censorious or arbitrary, rather be yielding and humble in your spirit and assert the truth by moral suasion and gentle fervor than by dogmatic force. Write as often as you can, not to interfere with your duties. A good letter to me will be one to all the family except Louie, who will expect to have her own correspondence from you. We want her to feel that your home is not broken up. Your rooms are at her service and command at any moment, and she is welcome to come and occupy them whenever and as long as she pleases. . . . She is a good girl, and we confidently expect the Lord will bless her and you so that you both shall accomplish a glorious mission in all its fulness on the earth, and I don't want either of you to feel the least discouraged in any possible way, but to continue to put your trust in the Lord and he will most assuredly open your way. I feel so confident in my spirit in making this promise that I would almost pronounce it an inspired prediction, but never mind, we will trust in the Lord and we feel sure that He will do all things right.

Joseph Fielding's mission proved to be a very difficult experience. "Despite diligent labors he did not make one convert, did not have opportunity to perform one baptism, although he did confirm one convert. It was enough to discourage the stoutest heart. He had heard of the days when the gospel was first introduced in England, when converts came in by the hundreds, sometimes by whole congregations. That was 60 years earlier. Times had indeed changed. Most of the few people there who were members of the Church were so apathetic toward it that it was sometimes necessary to cancel Sunday meeting for lack of attendance."[1]

Joseph Fielding returned from his mission on 9 July 1901, just a few months before Joseph F. was ordained President of the Church (a position he held for seventeen years, until his death in 1918). The future looked bright for Joseph Fielding and Louie; by 1906 they had two daughters—Josephine and Julina. Louie's pregnancies were difficult, however, and she suffered serious health problems during her third pregnancy, early in 1908. She steadily went downhill, with vomiting that doctors seemed helpless to stop. She died in March, at age thirty-one.

Joseph Fielding made the following entry in his journal: "During this month which has been one of constant anxiety and worry for me, I have passed through trials and experiences of the deepest and most painful kind. And through it all I have depended on the Lord for strength and comfort. After suffering most excruciating pain for three or four weeks and after an illness covering a period of nearly two months my beloved wife was released from her suffering Monday, March 30, 1908, and departed from me and our precious babies, for a better world, where we patiently and in sorrow await a meeting which shall be most glorious."[2]

A Father's Tender Expressions to His Daughter

CHARLES A. CALLIS TO KATHLEEN CALLIS LARSEN
10 DECEMBER 1927

By 1927, tireless missionaries Charles A. and Grace Pack Callis had been serving in the South for more than twenty years. Most of this time they were heading the mission. Though small in stature (five feet five inches), President Callis had a powerful personality; he was well known for his no-nonsense approach to missionary work and his energy. He supervised two hundred and fifty missionaries scattered throughout eleven states and urged them to tract at least four hours every day, to keep themselves well groomed, and to watch expenses. President Callis gave personal emphasis to the last point by being extremely frugal with mission funds—as he traveled throughout the huge mission, it was not uncommon for him to save money by sleeping on a train-station bench instead of checking into a motel for the night.

Charles Callis wrote the following letter to his second daughter, Kathleen, not long after she married Spencer Larsen. Brother Callis was sixty-two, and she was in her early twenties.

December 10, 1927

Dear Kathleen:

I arrived in Atlanta yesterday morning. The children* had gone to school, an evidence that they were in good health.

Your mother is missed.† The house or home is not complete without her. Laura is doing well as the housekeeper.

---

*Three children still remained with President and Sister Callis: Paul, Laura, and Pearl.

†Sister Callis had apparently been in Utah to help with Kathleen's weddding and to prepare for Grace's wedding.

We completed the series of conferences Wednesday at Richmond va. Bro. Whitney* left for Washington Thursday. He is writing very interesting letters to the Deseret News descriptive of the south, and he relates his experiences here. Four of his letters have appeared in the Saturday News. Have you read them? In one of his letters he pays a high and well deserved tribute to your dear mother. The last of his letters will be the one describing Richmond.

The conferences have been rich in spirituality, good fellowship, and they have been largely attended. Elder Whitney delivered eloquent and powerful discourses.

Just think, dear Kathleen, that three of you will not be with us this Christmas.† But we will all be "present in spirit," though absent in body. Your mother is busy preparing for Grace's wedding. Too bad that I am deprived of the happiness of witnessing the marriage ceremony, as I was your wedding.

Did you secure a refund on the Pullman? If you need any help in this matter let me aid you. First time I ever lost a RR ticket. I felt bad to leave you in that difficulty.

A pupil said to his teacher: "All the knowledge I have, I owe to you." The teacher replied: "Don't mention such a trifle." You ought to hear Bro. Whitney tell funny stories.

Be of good cheer, dear Kathleen. You will find that duty well and willingly performed brings the joy that endures. Treasures of

---

*Elder Orson F. Whitney, of the Quorum of the Twelve. E. R. Hamilton, district president in Durham, North Carolina, sent the following report of a December 4 conference to the *Improvement Era:* "Although stormy weather prevailed, the conference was well attended and all enjoyed a spiritual feast from the inspiring sermons delivered by Elder Orson F. Whitney, of the Council of the Twelve. It was indeed a pleasure to have a choice servant of the Lord at our conference. The elders in this district are working with great enthusiasm."

†The three oldest children: Grace, Kathleen, and Josephine.

the world are only wafers: joy that follows duty, as the harvest follows the planting, is as good home made bread.

"But pleasures are like poppies spread,
You seize the flower, the bloom is shed
Or like the snow flakes in the river:
One moment white, then gone forever."—Burns

A great writer has said that we must know the meaning of self sacrifice before we can win the crown of eternal life. I remember when I was on a mission [in] England, I read a verse that impressed me very much. I think the author of it is Coleridge. Here it is:

"This is a scene of combat, not of rest.
Man's life is a laborious one at best.
On this side death his labors never cease:
His joys are joys of conquest, not of peace."

The Lord bless you, my dear daughter. Be prayerful. Follow the example of your devoted mother. Emulate her virtues. She is using her splendid life for the good of her children, and also for many others outside the family circle.

I send my love and all good wishes to you and Spence.

Your affectionate father
Chas. A. Callis

⌒

Approximately three thousand missionaries served in the Southern States Mission under President and Sister Callis, among them Sterling W. Sill, who later served as an Assistant to the Quorum of the Twelve and as a member of the First Quorum of the Seventy from 1954 to 1978. The Callis children were all raised in the South, and the family shared happy memories of their time there, first in Chattanooga, Tennessee, and later in Atlanta, Georgia. They also experienced heartbreak when twins Charles Albert Callis and Nephi

Quilliam Callis, born 11 November 1907, both died at less than two months old: Nephi on 26 December and Charles on 27 December.

Charles Callis was called to the Quorum of the Twelve in October of 1933, and he and Grace left the South early in 1934. By that time, their youngest child was close to twenty years old. Throughout his tenure as an apostle, Elder Callis frequently answered mail from friends in the South seeking counsel. For the rest of their lives, he and Grace referred to the South as home.

"To You and Father Our Thoughts Go Continually"

JOHN A. WIDTSOE AND LEAH EUDORA DUNFORD
WIDTSOE TO SUSA YOUNG GATES
19 MARCH 1930

Born in Norway in 1872, John A. Widtsoe was fatherless at six. Not long after that, his mother converted to Mormonism. She brought her two boys to the United States when John was twelve and supported the family by working as a seamstress. John worked hard to educate himself, showing a particular aptitude for science.

In the early 1890s, John was accepted at Harvard University, and there he met Leah Eudora Dunford, who attended classes there one summer. She was the daughter of Susa Young Gates and granddaughter of Brigham Young. Like her mother, she was an accomplished writer. She and John were married in 1898 and soon departed for Goettigen, Germany, where John received his master's and Ph.D. degrees in chemistry from George Augustus University, one of the highest-rated universities in the world. (John attended on a Parker Fellowship from Harvard, where he had graduated *summa cum laude* with a bachelor's degree.)

John A. Widtsoe taught at Brigham Young University and Utah State Agricultural College and was president of the University of Utah. He published seven scientific books and more than seventy-five scientific papers on chemistry and agriculture. But his promising career in science and education took a different turn when he was called to the Quorum of the Twelve Apostles in 1921, at age forty-nine.

In 1928, the Widtsoes were called to England, where John served as president of the European Mission and Leah served as president of the Relief Societies of the European Mission. Two years later, when they were preparing for the 150th anniversary of the founding of the Church, John, fifty-eight, and

Leah, fifty-six, wrote the following letters to Leah's mother, Susa Young Gates, who had turned seventy-four the previous day. John and Leah both make reference to the *Life Story of Brigham Young*, coauthored by Susa and Leah. It was published in England later that same year (1930) by Jarrolds of London. The first letter that follows is from John; the second from Leah.

—

March 19th 1930
Mrs. Susa Y. Gates
672 North First West
Salt Lake City, Utah
U. S. A.
Dear Mother:

. . . You asked me some important questions in your note of March 3rd. I believe that the Prophet Joseph Smith actually saw the Father and the Son and talked with them as men talk together in the flesh; but that, undoubtedly, such communion between the boy and Divinity was made possible only by some transforming or protecting influence from the Lord, which made mortality endure the presence of immortality. It is because of the logical need of some such protective, enlightening, spiritualizing condition to permit communion with heavenly beings that so many of our thinkers have allowed themselves to be driven into the theory of a mental projection. It was a vision no doubt, but what is a vision? I should like to put the whole thing on paper sometime from my point of view. These are merely thoughts talked into the dictaphone. There are clues of full explanation of it in the Book of Moses, and in the Prophet's own statement concerning his various manifestations in the History of the Church. I cannot satisfy myself with the theory that the vision of Joseph Smith was merely subjective. It must have had objective realities. I can conceive it more than possible that another man standing by the side of Joseph, not touched with the same powers, would be unable to see what Joseph saw. That, however, does not in any degree destroy the reality of Joseph's vision.

Your May *Era* article* we have not seen. The *Saturday Evening Post* article arrived. Thank you very much. It is a splendid and accurate analysis of conditions as they exist here. I have not dared to write anything about conditions as between the various countries, because we are here to serve them all and there is no need of awakening antagonism. Conditions are pretty much as set forth in the *Saturday Evening Post*. Conditions are very bad in England—they could scarcely be worse. War thoughts are brewing. The people do not want war, but their leaders do.

We are right in the midst of our Centennial Celebration labor, and it is some labor. But, no need to speak of that.

I cannot tell you how much I appreciate your remembrance from time to time. It is a wonderful thing how deeply those of us over here may at times be forgotten. I have my hands full writing letters back and forth for samples of material issued, published and distributed at home, so that we may keep in step with the Church at large. That, however is only a natural result of human effort.

Meanwhile, the work is going on wonderfully well. Brigham Young's book is now in type and will be published in the course of a month. We have space in the International Hygiene Exposition for a Word of Wisdom exhibit, incredible as it seems. Radio and newspaper opportunities are multiplying. We are short of mature people to do the work required here. But, even as it is

---

*The article was entitled "Debunking the Debunkers of Scriptures." In her characteristic way, Susa Young Gates wrote: "Help me, dear Lord, to be patient with thy developing boys! Teach them the folly of the tearing down the walls of the Temple because of a tiny flaw in the structure. Give me charity! Give them common-sense!" (*Improvement Era*, May, 1930.)

the work is moving forward. I cannot help but believe, as I have said before, that the future is full of promise on this side of the Atlantic.

To you and Father* our thoughts [go] continually in affection and appreciation. If I have not written much of late it is because I have not had time to do more than a fraction of the required work placed upon me. We never fail to remember you, to pray for you and to send you our loving greetings.

All is well with us. News from Anna† and Lew is to the effect that they are to move back to Salt Lake City. Well, perhaps it is the right thing to do. They may have to meet financial adversity, but once they are over it they may be happier.

We send you our love.

Your son

John

⌐

Mother Darling,

I am so sorry that I was unable to get a long letter to you for your birthday. I didn't try to send you a present for it is so difficult to get things sent. If they go in the mail they are delayed so long, and then there is the nuisance of your probably having to pay duty on any small thing—and that doesn't seem like a present. Even the few things I sent home at Christmas: an Elder volunteered to take them for me and just recently billed me for $25.00 duty which he *said* he had to pay. But he rendered me no accounting—just gave it to me in a lump sum; and the whole trifling lot didn't cost me that much. We didn't send much of

---

*Jacob Forsberry Gates, Susa's second husband, who became Leah's stepfather when she was five years old. He died in 1942, nine years after Susa.

†The Widtsoes' older daughter, Anna Widtsoe Wallace.

50

anything this year to any one, except the $25.00 we sent to Cecil.* Beads, and a few trifles went to Anna—some to Rose and those to you—none of them expensive. So we decided that if you could you would have said don't send a thing; so we didn't—except a *load* of *love* which went with the cable. I hope you received that on "*the* day." We [thought] of you and talked of you frequently. I worked all day on B.Y. proof, Eudora† reading to me. This I hope will be the final. I've read and studied and arranged and rearranged so much that I practically know the manuscript by heart—word for word. It has taken much time, but if only you and the Brethren especially our dearest friends (the Presidency) feel satisfied, we shall feel more than repaid. For I'm sure it will be a powerful missionary. The first price will be too high I fear; but I think the Publishers intend to get out a cheaper edition later. Of that we have no control. We are doing our best. Love—

Leah

John and Leah served over the European Mission until 1933. (The president of the European Mission, usually an apostle, supervised all mission presidents in Europe. The European and British Missions were under one president until 1928, when, at Elder Widtsoe's suggestion, they were split.) Over the next twenty years, the Widtsoes lived a full life. Elder Widtsoe served as editor of the *Improvement Era*, director of the Genealogical Society of Utah, and commissioner of Church education. He advised the federal government on scientific matters and published more than twenty religious books and hundreds of articles and pamphlets.

Leah regularly published articles on such topics as Brigham Young, the

---

*Leah's younger brother, Cecil Gates.

†The Widtsoes' younger daughter, Leah Eudora Widtsoe. She later married future General Authority G. Homer Durham.

pioneers, and marriage. She wrote courses for the Mutual Improvement Association, produced a cookbook called *How to Be Well*, and coauthored a book on the Word of Wisdom with John. She served on the Board of Trustees for Brigham Young University.

John and Leah endured the deaths of five of their seven children. The first and last child—Anna and Leah—both lived long lives, but John Jr., Mark, Helen, and Mary all died in infancy, and Marsel died at age twenty-four in 1927. (Leah thus experienced the same kind of pain well known by her mother, Susa Young Gates, who survived eight of her thirteen children.) "Deep disappointment and sorrow ensued, but no bitterness," said Richard L. Evans at Elder Widtsoe's funeral in 1952. "Instead they took unto themselves yet other sons, whom they counseled and encouraged and lifted on their way in life. I thank my Father in heaven that I was one of them, and a host of others would so testify if it were their privilege to do so here today."

Elder Evans continued his tribute to John Widtsoe:

"No one may know the number he has helped. His heart, his home, were open to all, and when he was not at the office, those who sought him in solving personal problems beat a path to his home, even in his illness. . . .

"I cannot say how much we shall miss him. We shall miss his quick step. We shall miss the acute mind that quickly cut to the core of questions and problems presented. We shall miss stepping into his room, with his books and his tools of writing. We shall miss his kindly humor, his counsel, and his comfort and encouragement. We know not how much we shall miss him, but the years go quickly, and John A. Widtsoe is still himself, and should we ever come within reach of so high a place as where he is, we should like to take his outstretched hand and resume our talk where last we left it."[1]

"How Great and Wonderful a Father We Had"

ZINA YOUNG CARD TO SUSA YOUNG GATES
22 JANUARY 1931

Zina Young Card and Susa Young Gates were both daughters of Brigham Young, and both were in their twenties when Brigham died. Like their father, both were strong willed and dedicated to the faith. There are a number of other interesting similarities between them. Both married twice: Zina's first husband, Thomas Williams (twenty-one years her senior), died when she was twenty-four, and she married Charles Ora Card ten years later; Susa divorced her first husband, Alma Bailey Dunford, when she was twenty-one and married Jacob Forsberry Gates when she was twenty-three. Both women had two children at the time they remarried, and both had additional children with their second husbands. Both had sons-in-law who became apostles—Zina's daughter Zina Card married Hugh B. Brown; Susa's daughter Leah Eudora Dunford married John A. Widtsoe.

Not long after her first husband's death, Zina went with her brother and her two young boys to Sevier County, where she built a log cabin, fenced the property, and planted trees. One night the wind was so fierce that she and her sons were unable to light a candle.

Almost ten years later she married Charles Card. This was followed by a trek to Canada and years of living in harsh conditions. John D. Higginbotham, western Canada pioneer and writer, wrote of Zina:

"One of the most outstanding characters of the Mormon settlements, Mrs. Charles Ora Card (affectionately known as 'Aunt Zina') was an early guest at my home. She was, I think she informed me, a daughter of the third wife of Brigham Young,* the famous founder of Salt Lake City and their

---

*Zina's mother, Zina Dinatha Huntington Young, was one of eight women sealed to Brigham during 1846, at a time when he already had six wives. Young Zina was the only child born to Brigham and Zina Huntington. Susa was the second child born to Brigham and Lucy Bigelow, who were sealed in 1847.

colonies in Utah, and inherited much of his energy and ability. One evening she spent hours in my library discussing religion and other themes, searching the scriptures and consulting many books of reference until tables and chairs were covered with them. We debated many questions, drew our own conclusions and parted the best of friends. . . . Mrs. Card was a fluent and convincing speaker, as well as a woman of grace and charm, and exercised a far-reaching influence on the life of Southern Alberta."[1]

Susa showed similar drive and ability: she founded the department of music at Brigham Young Academy and also founded the *Young Woman's Journal*. She published novels and biographies, served as press chairman of the National Council of Women, and edited the *Relief Society Magazine* for many years. One historian called Susa "the most versatile and prolific LDS writer ever to take up the pen in defense of her religion."[2]

In 1931, Zina Presendia[3] Young Williams Card, "Aunt Zina," was eighty years old; she had been a widow (for the second time) since Charles Ora Card's death in 1906, at age sixty-six. She was in LDS Hospital in Salt Lake City when she wrote the following letter to her half-sister, Susa Young Gates, seventy-four.

———

L. D. S. Hospital. Jan 22 1931
City.
Mrs. Susa Y. Gates,
Dear Sister Susa,

I have been in receipt of your letter some time. Have not answered as I was promised a reporter to come and help me. My eye is better today, and I am sending a reply to your request. By the way, you did not include Clint's letter.

My loved Sister Susa,

I have not had the privilege of reading your priceless book,* you know why. As you are the author of its pages, you certainly

---

*Life Story of Brigham Young, which had been published in England the previous year.

54

have the privilege of seeing facts from your standpoint, and as I could not write it, I hereby feel to endorse your subject matter as being strictly authentic, and am proud and thankful, that after 50 years, the family, who have grown to manhood and womanhood, can see life from our lives and our mothers', how great and wonderful a father we had, and such good, true women our mothers were.

There is only one Susa in our family, and I endorse "her." God bless her.

Your constant friend and admiring sister,

Zina Young Card

If you felt I was worth a few moments of your time* it would be appreciated by your sister who has outlived her usefulness.

Zina Young Card

———

Nine days after she wrote this letter, Zina Young Card died—on 31 January 1931. She was survived by four of her five children. Susa Young Gates devoted much of her time in her final years to genealogy work. She wrote genealogy columns for newspapers, produced genealogy manuals, compiled a systematic name index for the Church, and personally cataloged more than 16,000 names of the Young family. In addition, she and her husband, Jacob Gates, were temple workers in the Salt Lake Temple. In May of 1933, just a little over two years after the above letter was written, Susa Young Gates died at age seventy-seven.[†]

---

*Susa responded with a letter saying she would not be able to visit the hospital at that time; the two sisters therefore probably did not see each other again before Zina died.

[†]The last of Brigham Young's surviving children, Rhoda Mabel (a sister to Susa) and Fannie (daughter of Mary Van Cott), died in 1950, both in their eighties.

Advice to a Fifteen-Year-Old Son

JOSEPH FIELDING SMITH TO LEWIS SMITH
24 JANUARY 1934

Lewis Warren Smith was the second of five sons* born to Joseph Fielding Smith and Ethel Georgina Reynolds (the daughter of George Reynolds, a member of the First Council of the Seventy). The five boys—Joseph, Lewis, Reynolds, Douglas, and Milton—grew up with a father who encouraged them in both music and sports. Joseph Sr. could defeat any of his boys in handball—with either hand. The boys also played chess and checkers with their dad.

Joseph Sr. was a prompt man who always left for work by 7:30, walking to his office in the Church Administration Building. When the children were old enough for school, they would walk with their father, and he always parted by kissing them good-bye.

Joseph Sr. was fifty-seven and had been an apostle for twenty-four years when he wrote the following letter to Lewis, fifteen.

My Dear Lewis:—

I have just written a letter to your oldest brother who is in England,† and I thought that it would not be out of place for me to write a letter to you also, for you, being at home, do not get many letters. I was thinking that we have sent one boy away to try to teach the gospel to people in the world, and that the people

---

*When the Smiths's newspaper carrier, Stanley Dixon, was orphaned at about twelve years of age, relatives took in his brothers and sisters, but the Smiths invited Stanley to live with them. He accepted the invitation and lived with the Smiths until he reached maturity.

†Joseph Fielding Smith III, who was twenty-three when this letter was written. He served as a missionary in England from 1933–35 and was president of the Liverpool District for the last sixteen months of his mission. All five sons of Joseph Fielding and Ethel Smith served honorable missions.

here at home need it just as much as do the people in foreign lands. The world is full of theories, philosophies, and all kinds of doctrines, and people are being led astray. I wonder if I am putting forth the proper effort by example and by precept, to instruct my own children so that they will understand the truth and have the power to overcome the temptations and sins of the world. An ancient prophet said that in these last days the devil would rage in the hearts of the people; that he would be stirred up to anger against that which is good. Some people he would lull away into false security until they were bound by the chains of hell. (See 2 Nephi 28.) The Lord told Joseph Smith that there were many spirits abroad in the land (D&C 50:1–3.) and that some spirits or doctrines are the commandments of men and others of devils. (D&C 46:7.)

Another ancient prophet said that in the last days men would be lovers of pleasure more than lovers of God; they would be disobedient (2 Tim. 3:1–7) and they would be ever learning and never able to come to a knowledge of the truth. They would be sent "fables" because they would not receive the truth, and "strong delusions." (2 Tim. 4:3–4.) They would have their consciences seared with a hot iron (1 Tim. 4:1–2.) and would follow seducing spirits and doctrines of devils. (Thessalonians 2:11.) In this manner, and there are many other passages containing prophetic sayings of this kind, the Lord has warned us so that we may escape from all these things if we will only treasure up his word. (Pearl of Great Price page 47.) The light of the Spirit of the Lord will keep us in the path so that we shall have power to recognize evil and segregate it from the truth if we will only do the will of the Lord. He who will not do his will is deceived until the time comes when he is bound by the chains of hell.

Now, I am somewhat concerned over the school work of my

children, for I know that they are taught all kinds of theories, as we never were taught before, which have a tendency to destroy faith and make people deny the power of God. You cannot be too careful in matters of this kind. I want to protect you and each of the children from these attacks and cunningly laid plans of Lucifer to destroy faith in the Son of God and the redemption of man.

I sense keenly the dangers which confront my children and all other children at this day. You do not sense it because you have not had the training and experience, so I want to help you. Let me say that I KNOW that Joseph Smith spoke the truth. It is not a question of guessing or belief, just as you know that 2 added to 2 will equal 4. I know that Jesus Christ is the Only Begotten Son of God, and the Redeemer of the world. What a glorious thing it is to know this! How soul satisfying it is! What peace and comfort it brings to me! I want *you* to know it also, and you may if you seek.

I want you to be true to your priesthood, and one day you will have the higher priesthood conferred upon you. I want you to live to be a teacher of men in the everlasting truth, not the truth which the world knows, and which is mixed with error. The pride, wisdom and prudence of the great men of the world will have to pass away; but the *truth* which comes from God will never pass away for it is eternal.

I am depending on you to learn these things for yourself and teach them to your younger brothers. I depend upon you, you must not fail me! What ever else you do be true to your Father which is in heaven. Have I ever set you an example in unrighteousness? Have you ever known me to lie? to steal? to wilfully bear false witness? to be unclean in body and in mind? I want you to remember that you have descended through the lineage of prophets! Your fathers before you, not counting your own father, have been mighty men of God. Your grandfather was always true, and would have laid down his life for the gospel. He gave his life *to* it, and would have given it *for* it, in fact sacrificed his time and comfort for it. Your great-grandfather not only suffered persecution, trials and tribulations, but he did give his life for the gospel truth. These were noble men. I want you to so live that you will be a credit to them, and if you can an improvement on your father.

Now, you may not fully appreciate this letter now. I want you to save it and someday you may read it with greater care and understanding. Be true to me, true to your mother, true to the Church and true to God! . . .

Lewis made plans to serve a mission, just as his father hoped, and received his mission call during the summer of 1937, when he was nineteen. Shortly after the call came, Lewis's mother, Ethel Reynolds Smith, who had suffered frail health for several years, died of a cerebral hemorrhage at age forty-seven. Her death made Joseph Fielding Smith a widower for the second time. Elder Smith and Lewis therefore experienced a poignant mix of joy and sorrow when Lewis left on his mission to Switzerland a month and a half after his mother's funeral.

From May to October of 1939, Elder Smith and his third wife, Jesse Evans Smith (whom he had married in April of 1938) toured missions throughout Britain and Europe. They attended a mission presidents' conference in Switzerland in June and were able to see Lewis, who met his stepmother, Jesse, for the first time. The mission presidents who attended the conference, including Hugh B. Brown of the British Mission, were deeply concerned about the threat of war. Tensions continued to mount, and on 1 September 1939, Hitler invaded Poland. By the end of the month, most American missionaries serving in Europe had been sent home. Lewis, secretary to Swiss Mission President Thomas E. McKay, was one of the last to leave.

Like his brothers Reynolds and Douglas, Lewis served in the military during World War II. He achieved the rank of staff sergeant and served in India and Africa in the Army Intelligence Service. He spent Christmas of 1944 in Bethlehem and mailed a postcard from there to his family. He was expected back in the United States soon. The same day the family received the postcard, however, they also received a telegram informing them that Lewis had been killed in action. His plane had exploded in midair; sabotage was suspected. He was twenty-six.

In a letter to his daughter and son-in-law, Lois and William S. Fife, Elder Smith wrote, "One thing that helps us is the fact that each of the men who has written to us has testified to Lewis' clean life, his high principles and his integrity to his religion. When each writes this way, without any consultation, it is a great tribute to our boy, son and brother. . . . Such words as these are comforting, and each has testified in the same manner about him. The beautiful thing about it all is that it is so true. A better boy could not be found. A more worthy one could not be taken. We are sure that he was called to some work on the other side."[1]

"She Has Been the Perfect Lady"

DAVID O. MCKAY TO HIS SONS AND DAUGHTERS
25 OCTOBER 1934

When Anthony W. Ivins, first counselor to Heber J. Grant, died on 23 September 1934, Apostle David O. McKay spoke at his funeral. "After the return from the cemetery," he recorded, "Pres. Heber J. Grant called me by telephone, and requested me to call on him at his residence. On this occasion, he informed [me] that he had chosen me to succeed Pres. Ivins in the First pres. The call coming so suddenly, I was entirely overcome. After an extended interview, when I arose to leave, he put his arms around me and kissed me."[1]

David was sustained as second counselor at the October conference, at age sixty-one (with J. Reuben Clark Jr. moving from second counselor to first counselor). Three weeks later, he wrote the following letter to his children:

Salt Lake City, Utah,
October 25, 1934
To my beloved Sons and Daughters—
David L. and Mildred,
Llewelyn R. and Alice,
Lou Jean and Russell,
Emma Rae,
Edward R. and
Robert R.
—children, not one of whom has ever done a thing to cause their parents sorrow, but who in their consideration, devotion and achievement have filled our hearts with justifiable pride and gratitude.

61

Dear David L. and Mildred:

Recently there came to me the highest honor and greatest responsibility of my life. I am not unmindful of what this appointment to the First Presidency of the Church means to us as a family. I am sure you also appreciate this and share willingly and conscientiously whatever added responsibility the Call may place upon you.

Aptly it has been said that, "Often a woman shapes the career of husband, or brother, or son. A man succeeds and reaps the honors of public applause, when in truth a quiet little woman has made it all possible—has by her tact and encouragement held him to his best, has had faith in him when his own faith has languished, has cheered him with the unfailing assurance 'you can, you must, you will.'"

I need not tell you children how fittingly this tribute applies to your mother. All through the years you have seen how perfectly she fills the picture. There is not a line or a touch but is applicable. For over thirty-three years, I have realized this, and each of you has known it to a greater or less degree as many years as your ages indicate; but like the Scotchman who "cam' near tellin' his wife ance or twice" that he loved her, we have not told mother of her loving worth and inspiration to us.

Recently, since October 6th particularly,* I have had a yearning to see my father and mother† just to tell them what their lives, their daily example, and willing sacrifices for their children have meant to me. I want to acknowledge to them my unpayable

---

*The day he was sustained to the First Presidency.

†David O. McKay's mother, Jennette Evans McKay, died in 1905, at age fifty-four; his father, David McKay, died in 1917, at age seventy-three.

debt of eternal gratitude. But they are not here, and I must await an opportunity in the distant Future.

Your mother is here—well and happy and as sweet and charming in life's afternoon* as she was in the morning of beautiful womanhood. I want to acknowledge to you and to her, how greatly her loving devotion, inspiration, and loyal support have contributed to whatever success may be ours.

Willingly and ably she has carried the responsibility of the household.

Uncomplainingly she has economized when our means have been limited—and that has been the case nearly all our lives.

Always prompt with meals, she has never said an unpleasant word or even shown a frown when I have kept her waiting, sometimes for hours.

If I had to take a train at midnight or later, she would either sit up with me or lie awake to make sure that I should not oversleep.

If duty required me to leave at five o'clock in the morning, she was never satisfied unless she could prepare me a bite of breakfast before I left home.

It has been mother who remembered the birthdays and purchased the Christmas presents.

Since January 2, 1901, the happy day when she became my bride, she has never given me a single worry except when she was ill and that has been, with few exceptions, only with the responsibilities of motherhood.

Thus my mind has been remarkably free to center upon the problems, cares, and requirements incident to my duties and responsibilities.

In sickness, whether it was one of you or I, her untiring

*Emma Ray Riggs McKay was fifty-seven when this letter was written.

attention night and day was devotion personified; her practical skill, invariably effective; and her physical endurance, seemingly unlimited. Many an ache and pain she has endured in uncomplaining silence so as not to give the least worry to the loved one to whom she was giving such tender care.

Sometimes I have come home tired and irritable and have made remarks provocative of retaliating replies; but never to this day have you heard your mother say a cross or disrespectful word. This can be said truthfully, I think, of but few women in the world.

Under all conditions and circumstances, she has been the perfect lady.

Her education has enabled her to be a true helpmate; her congeniality and interest in my work, a pleasing companion; her charm and unselfishness, a lifelong sweetheart; her unbounded patience and intelligent insight to childhood, a most devoted mother;—these and many other virtues combined with her loyalty and self-sacrificing devotion to her husband, impel me to crown her the sweetest, most helpful, most inspiring sweetheart and wife that ever inspired a man to noble endeavor.

To her we owe our happy family life and whatever success we may have achieved!

I know you love her and, oh how she loves each one of you!

Hundreds of letters and telegrams from friends, acquaintances and even strangers—members and non-members of the Church in all walks of life have brought congratulatory messages, prayerful wishes for success and assurances of confidence and loyal support for which I am indeed sincerely grateful.

I have noted with joy that in many of these messages your loving mother is included in the congratulations and commendations expressed. I want at least her loved ones to know that she rightfully shares in *all* achievements and honors.

Happy he

With such a mother! Faith in womankind

Beats with his blood, and trust in all things high

Comes easy to him, and though he trip and fall

He shall not bind his soul with clay.

But one on earth is better than the wife;

*that is mother.**

With loving devotion and appreciation of your love and loyalty, I remain as always

Your affectionate

Daddy

David O. McKay and Emma Ray Riggs were married in 1901. Five years later, at the age of thirty-two, David was ordained an apostle. Over the next half century, he and Emma Ray shared an incredibly rich life together as David served as an apostle for sixty-three years and nine months, longer than any other man.†

The couple, who had seven children, celebrated their sixty-ninth anniversary on 2 January 1970. "On January 18, 1970," wrote their son David Lawrence McKay, "at age ninety-six, [David O. McKay] died quietly in his Hotel Utah apartment with Mother and their children present. Mother lingered on, sweet and uncomplaining, for ten months. None of us ever heard

---

*From a poem by Alfred, Lord Tennyson.

†Heber J. Grant and Joseph Fielding Smith were the only other apostles to serve for more than sixty years. Elder Grant served for sixty-two years, seven months; Elder Smith served for sixty-two years, three months.

her merry peal of laughter again after Father's death, although she always greeted us with her warm smile and loving caresses. When she slipped away on 14 November 1970, despite our heartache, none of us would have delayed that last, permanent reunion with her beloved sweetheart."[2]

"Together You Can Dream Dreams"

HAROLD B. LEE TO HELEN LEE GOATES
21 NOVEMBER 1946

In 1946, forty-seven-year-old Harold B. Lee, previously the impressive managing director of the Church welfare program, had been a member of the Quorum of the Twelve for five years. He and his wife, Fern Tanner Lee, had two daughters, twenty-two-year-old Maurine and twenty-year-old Helen. Elder and Sister Lee were surprised, but still supportive, when Helen announced that she was engaged to L. Brent Goates, a serviceman she had dated for only one week. Elder Lee performed the temple sealing on 24 June 1946, calling it one of the greatest experiences of his life. Two weeks later, Brent returned to military service. He and Helen were reunited briefly in Portland, Oregon, in November. Elder Lee, then on a Church assignment, wrote the following letter to his daughter on motel stationery in Mesa, Arizona.

My dearest baby,

This is intended to be something of a birthday letter to my "youngest" from a sentimental old Dad who is lonesome for his lovely daughter. So far as I can recall this is the first time in your life that you will be spending your birthday* and Thanksgiving away from us, and, with the exception of the year we were in Mexico, the first time away from your home on those days.

As with every day of your life, you can never relive any part of it except in memory and if any day be wasted or misspent, that

---

*Helen would turn twenty-one four days later, on 25 November 1946.

day becomes only one of regret or remorse. To live one's life to the fullest then becomes a daily responsibility for which you need the constant guidance of divine powers to avoid the pitfalls that make for long detours back onto the path of safety and truth. Too many adopt the philosophy of the old preacher "unless you are in desperate need, your prayers just ain't got no suction." One who has understanding realizes that we are always in great need of spiritual help. So it was that the Master taught:

"Blessed are the poor in spirit who come unto me, for theirs is the Kingdom of Heaven."*

The "poor in spirit" are the spiritually needy who daily lean on and trust the arm of the Lord.

To me your birthday, always on or about Thanksgiving Day, has always seemed most appropriate. I thanked God for my baby when you came 21 years ago and I have thanked him for you every day since. From babyhood you have possessed strong opinions and a will. Well do I remember your childhood efforts to make it an obedient will and my prayer, today, as always in the past, [for you is that] your will be made subservient to that which is right. As the depth of your thinking has been revealed on many occasions when you have furnished us keepsakes of your thinking, I have gloried in the unfolding of the life of my own daughter. When you made the greatest decision of your life thus far, in choosing your life's companion, somehow I had complete assurance that you had chosen well. My own way would have been to have urged greater deliberation, but perhaps the times justified the means and I accepted your decision with thanksgiving.

There lies yet ahead greater joys and, yes, greater anxieties than you have yet known for remember that great love is built on

---

*A reference to Matthew 5:3 but not an exact quote.

great sacrifice and that a daily determination in each other to please in things that are right will build a sure foundation for a happy home. That determination for the welfare of each other must be mutual and not one-sided or selfish. Husband and wife must feel equal responsibilities and obligations to each other. Two of the things that today [strike] at the security of modern homes is that young husbands have never sensed their full obligation in supporting a family and young wives have side-stepped the responsibility of settling down to the serious business of raising a family and making a home.

Your being with Brent now should prove a great blessing to both of you. Together you can dream dreams and together you can work and sacrifice to make your dreams come true. With all my love to you and Brent and wishing you much joy on your birthday, I am,

Your loving daddy,
Harold B. Lee

21 November 1946

—

Brent and Helen Goates were blessed with six children, and they were both active in Church and community. Brent served as a bishop and stake president and worked as administrator of LDS Hospital in Salt Lake City. Helen served twice as a member of the Relief Society general board, as well as a member of the Daughters of the Utah Pioneers and president of Sigma Chi Mother's Club.

From 1975 to 1978, Helen accompanied Brent as he presided over the California Arcadia Mission. Sister Goates died in April of 2000 at age seventy-four.

During the 1960s, Elder Lee, second in seniority to Joseph Fielding Smith in the Quorum of the Twelve, proposed a sweeping reorganization of Church programs and auxiliaries to focus more closely on priesthood leadership. This effort became known as "correlation." Just as he had been instrumental in the welfare program, Elder Lee headed the correlation program.

During these same years, however, Elder Lee and his family experienced dual sorrows. Fern Lee, who had had health problems for several years, died on 24 September 1962 at age sixty-six. Just three years later, Elder Lee's older daughter, Maurine Lee Wilkins, died suddenly of a lung embolus while expecting her fifth child. She was forty years old. The two remaining members of the original family—Elder Lee and Helen—grew even closer through these trials. From that time on, Elder Lee showed a remarkable ability to comfort those who had lost loved ones. He became President of the Church in 1972.

Part 3

~

"Fellow Citizens with the Saints"

FRIENDS
IN ZION

"A Book, About to Be Printed"

In the fall of 1828, a serious, slightly built young man from Vermont by the name of Oliver Cowdery began teaching school in the Palmyra, New York, area. Joseph Smith and his wife, Emma, were then living one hundred and thirty miles away in Harmony, Pennsylvania. Oliver soon heard rumors about the "Gold Bible" (including mention of it from one David Whitmer), and when he boarded with the Joseph Sr. family, he asked about those rumors. Wary because of the public furor created when Joseph obtained the plates a year earlier, Joseph Sr. said little. Oliver persisted however, eventually gaining the Smiths's confidence and hearing their account of young Joseph's experiences.

Lucy Mack Smith recorded that Oliver "was highly delighted with what he had heard, that he had been in a deep study upon the subject all day, and that it was impressed upon his mind, that he should yet have the privilege of writing for Joseph." Not long after that, Oliver told Lucy: "The subject upon which we were yesterday conversing seems working in my very bones, and I cannot, for a moment, get it out of my mind. . . . I shall make my arrangements to be ready to accompany [Samuel to Harmony], . . . for I have made it a subject of prayer, and I firmly believe that it is the will of the Lord that I should go."[1]

In the cold spring of 1829, Samuel Smith and Oliver Cowdery made the hard trip to Harmony, braving freezing rain and trudging over roads that alternately froze and thawed. Finally, on 5 April, Oliver and Joseph met for the first time. Two days later they began the work of translation, with Joseph dictating while looking at the Urim and Thummim or seer stone, inside his hat and Oliver transcribing.* Despite interruptions and a move back to New York (where they translated at the Whitmer home in Fayette), they produced a six-hundred-page manuscript—the text of the present Book of Mormon—in less than three months.

By August they had arranged for Grandin's printshop in Palmyra to print 5,000 copies of the Book of Mormon. With Oliver and Hyrum taking charge of the printing, Joseph returned to Harmony. Joseph wrote the following letter to Oliver two and a half weeks after he arrived there. They were both twenty-three years old.

—

Harmony [Pennsylvania]—Oct. 22, 1829

Respected Sir,

I would inform you that I arrived at home on sunday morning the 4th[,] after having a prosperous journey, and found all well. The people are all friendly to us except a few who are in opposition[†] to everything unless it is something that is exactly like themselves. Two of our most formidable persecutors are now under censure and are cited to a trial in the church for crimes which if true are worse than all the Gold Book business. We do not rejoice in the affliction of our enemies, but we shall be glad to have truth prevail.

There begins to be a great call for our books in this country; the minds of the people are very much excited when they find that there is a copyright obtained and that there is really a book, about to be printed. I have bought a horse of Mr. [Josiah]

---

*Although Joseph and Oliver said little about the actual method of translation, Emma Smith and David Whitmer both described it in detail. For example, see Emma's account in *Saints' Herald*, 1 Oct. 1879, 289–90; and David's account in Cook, *David Whitmer Interviews*, 72.

[†]Among the Harmony residents who opposed Joseph were Emma's uncle Nathaniel Lewis and his sons Joseph and Hiel.

Stowell* and want someone to come after it as soon as convenient. Mr. Stowell has a prospect of getting five or six hundred dollars; he does not know certain that he can get it, but he is a going to try and if he can get the money he wants to pay it in immediately for books.

We want to hear from you and know how you prosper in the good work. Give our best respects to Father and Mother and all our brothers and Sisters, to Mr. [Martin] Harris† and all the company concerned. Tell them that our prayers are put up daily for them that they may be prospered in every good word and that they may be preserved from sin here and from the consequence of sin hereafter. And now dear brother, be faithful in the discharge of every duty, looking for the reward of the righteous, and now may God of his infinite mercy keep and preserve us spotless until his coming and receive us all to rest with him in eternal repose through the atonement of Christ our Lord, Amen.

Joseph Smith, Jr.

Oliver H. Cowdery

―

Two or three months after writing this letter, Joseph had to return to Palmyra when newspaper editor Abner Cole (using the pseudonym Obadiah Dogberry) began illegally publishing extracts from 1 Nephi and Alma. (Cole had access to these extracts because his newspaper, *The Reflector*, was

---

*Joseph had known Josiah Stowell (sometimes spelled "Stoal") since 1825, when he and several others had helped Stowell search for reported Spanish treasure near Harmony. Joseph met Emma Hale while working for Stowell, and Stowell and Joseph Knight Sr. had both been present at the Smith home when Joseph received the plates in September of 1827.

†Martin Harris, the first of the Three Witnesses to become acquainted with the Smith family, befriended Joseph Smith as early as 1827 and helped Joseph protect the plates. He served as scribe during April–June of 1828 but lost 116 manuscript pages of the Book of Mormon.

published in Grandin's printshop.) Cole, who said he found nothing "treasonable" in the Book of Mormon, ceased after Joseph confronted him.

The process of printing the Book of Mormon continued throughout the fall and winter of 1829–30. John H. Gilbert,* who worked in Grandin's printshop, said that "Martin Harris, Hyrum Smith, and Oliver Cowdery, were very frequent visitors to the office during the printing of the Mormon Bible. The manuscript was supposed to be in the handwriting of Cowdery. Every Chapter, if I remember correctly, was one solid paragraph, without a punctuation mark, from beginning to end. Names of persons and places were generally capitalized, but sentences had no end. . . . I punctuated it to make it read as I supposed the Author intended, and but very little punctuation was altered in proofreading. . . . Cowdery held and looked over the manuscript when most of the proofs were read."[2]

On 26 March 1830, the *Wayne Sentinel* newspaper announced that the Book of Mormon was now for sale. Two weeks later, Joseph organized the Church; he and Oliver were two of the first six members.

---

*Although Gilbert recounted these events fifty years later, his memory seems to have been quite accurate (see Skousen).

"I Have Cherished a Hope"

OLIVER COWDERY TO PHINEAS H. YOUNG
23 MARCH 1846

On 12 April 1838, the high council* in Far West, Missouri, brought nine charges against Oliver Cowdery. These included "urging on vexatious Lawsuits," "seeking to destroy the character of President Joseph Smith," "not attending meetings," and "betaking himself to the beggerly elements of the world and neglecting his high and Holy Calling." Oliver's response was read at the same meeting. It said, in part: "This attempt to controll me in my temporal interests, I conceive to be a disposition to take from me a portion of my Constitutional privileges and inherent rights. I only, respectfully, ask leave, therefore to withdraw from a society assuming they have such right." Oliver made it clear, however, that his disagreements all related to the "outward government of this Church." After further discussion, the council excommunicated† the Church's second elder and cofounder.[1]

Oliver left Missouri and spent the next ten years in Ohio and Wisconsin, where he became a respected attorney. During his time out of the Church, he stayed in touch with his good friend Phineas H. Young, older brother to Brigham and husband of Oliver's younger sister Lucy. Just as Phineas had been a missionary to his brother Brigham (after obtaining a copy of the Book of

---

*The high council at that time included Samuel H. Smith, who had accompanied Oliver on a journey from Palmyra, New York, to Harmony, Pennsylvania (in the spring of 1829), where Oliver met Joseph Smith for the first time.

†Concerning his excommunication, Oliver wrote to Brigham Young in 1843: "Ambitious and wicked men, envying the harmony existing between myself and the first elders of the Church . . . caused all this difficulty from the beginning to end. They succeeded in getting myself out of the Church; but since they themselves have gone to perdition, ought not old friends—long tried in the furnace of affliction, to be friends still." (Oliver Cowdery to Brigham Young, 25 December 1843, Huntington Library; cited in Cannon and Cook, *Far West Record*, 170.)

Mormon from Samuel H. Smith), he now sought ways to bring Oliver back into the fold. In the following letter, written while he was still out of the Church, Oliver shows how seriously he took his responsibility as a witness of the Book of Mormon.

—

Tiffin, Seneca County, Ohio, March 23, 1846

Dear Brother Phineas:

Yours of the 5th and 9th mailed on the 11th has been received. I was not looking for a letter from you, nor did I expect, when one should be received that it would contain what yours does. I mean that part relative 2nd Eldership, Counselorship and (etc.).

Before the receipt of this, you will have received one from me, enclosed in another to Brother Daniel,* from which you will discover that your last was perused with the deepest satisfaction, and that one received from Brother Orson Hyde, about the same time, was either misunderstood, or in spirit misconceived by me. But from your last I am fully satisfied that no unjust imputation will be suffered to remain upon my character. And that I may not be misunderstood, let me here say, that I have only sought, and only asked, that my character might be exonerated from those charges imputed to me the crimes of theft, forgery, etc. Those which all my former associates know to be false. I do not, I have never asked, to be excused, or exempted from an acknowledgment of any actual fault or wrong—for of these there are many, which it always was my pleasure to confess—I have cherished a hope, and that one of my fondest, that I might leave such a character as those who might believe in my testimony, after I should be called hence, might do so, not only for the sake of the truth, but might not blush for the private character of the man who

---

*Oliver's brother-in-law, Daniel Jackson.

bore that testimony. I have been sensitive on this subject, I admit, but I ought to so be, you would be under the circumstances, had you stood in the presence of John with our departed Brother Joseph, to receive the lesser priesthood, and in the presence of Peter, to receive the greater, and looked down through time, and witness the effects these two must produce—you would feel what you have never felt, were wicked men conspiring to lessen the effects of your testimony on man, after you should have gone to your long sought rest. But, enough of this. I will here say, that I cannot fully comprehend the purpose of Brother Hyde's letter, but from your last, in referring to a conversation by Brother Brigham [Young] about the presidency, I am fully, doubly satisfied that all will be right—that my character will be fully vindicated. I write thus plainly because I do not intend to mention it again in any of my letters. Let the records show what you, Brother Parley [Pratt] and Brigham, think and they shall and you will be furnished with weapons to use against your enemies hereafter, to good effect.

You say you are having a meeting on the 6th of April. Brother Phineas, I could be with you, and tell you about the 6th of April 1830, when but six men then only belonged to the Church, and how we looked forward to a future. I should gladly, but I cannot only in spirit—but in spirit I shall be with you. And then in assembled kneel with those who are yet alive of that six. How many can you count?*

From my letters, you and Brother Daniel, you will see that Brother Thurstin left, much to my regret, without letting me see him again. I think if he were to send me a note that falls due the first of October 1846, I could get the money on it by giving a share; by this means I could be with you sooner than I know in

---

*Of the six original members of the Church—Oliver Cowdery, Hyrum Smith, Joseph Smith Jr., Samuel H. Smith, David Whitmer, and Peter Whitmer Jr.—only two, Oliver and David, were still alive.

any other way. You will, of course, see him on the subject, and I will too on receipt of this—the condition of my family is such that it is not possible for me to come with them, this spring, but I want to be prepared at the earliest moment.

We are well as usual. I write in great haste may the Lord God our Fathers bless you and yours—and the children as a body. Such is my prayer—such is my heart.

I am yours in the new and everlasting covenant.

Elder PG H. Young

William could dictate that the subject matter of our communication remain with the Twelve for the present. Our love to Daniel and Lucy and Phoebe.* Let me hear from you.

Oliver Cowdery

To: PG H. Young, Esq., Nauvoo, Hancock County, Illinois

Two and a half years after writing this letter, Oliver Cowdery, his wife, Elizabeth Whitmer Cowdery (sister to David Whitmer), and their daughter Maria Louise† left Elkhorn, Wisconsin, and traveled to Council Bluffs, Iowa. On 21 October, Oliver addressed a Church conference. "I wrote, with my own pen," he told them, "the entire Book of Mormon (save a few pages) as it fell from the lips of the Prophet Joseph Smith, as he translated it by the gift and power of God, by the means of the Urim and Thummim. . . . I beheld with my eyes, and handled with my hands,‡ the gold plates from which it was

---

*Lucy and Phoebe were Oliver's two youngest sisters (technically half-sisters, along with Rebecca Marie, because their mother was Keziah Pearce, whom William Cowdery had married after the death of Oliver's mother, Rebecca Fuller). Lucy was married to Phineas Young, and Phoebe was married to Daniel Jackson.

†Five other children died in infancy.

‡Since David Whitmer makes it clear that he and Oliver did not handle the plates when they saw the angel Moroni, Oliver must have handled the plates some other time, possibly when he attempted to translate.

translated. . . . That book is true. Sidney Rigdon did not write it; Mr. Spaulding did not write it. I wrote it myself, as it fell from the lips of the Prophet."[2]

Three weeks later, on Sunday, 12 November 1848, a decade after his excommunication, Oliver was rebaptized by Orson Hyde, president of the Quorum of the Twelve and one of the original apostles selected by Oliver, David Whitmer, and Martin Harris in 1835. Although Oliver planned to bring his family west, he was already suffering from a lung ailment, possibly chronic pulmonary tuberculosis. The condition steadily worsened, and on 3 March 1850 Oliver's wife, his daughter, Phineas and Lucy Young, David Whitmer, Hiram Page, and others gathered around Oliver's bed in the Peter Whitmer Sr. home in Richmond, Missouri, to say their last good-byes. "After shaking hands with the family and kissing David Whitmer and daughter, he said, 'Now I lay me down for the last time; I am going to meet my Savior,' and he died immediately with a smile on his face."[3]

"There Is Work for Me to Do Yet"

GEORGE ALBERT SMITH TO REED SMOOT
9 APRIL 1912

George Albert Smith's biographer states that George "came into the world with a handicap that was unknown to his father and his grandfather.* Nature denied him the kind of robust physique that was generally associated with leadership in the vigorous young civilization of the West, and it seemed most unlikely he could match the attainment of his forbears. Yet the fiery furnace of experience was to fuse in him a special kind of strength that would make history for his people."[1]

As a young man, George worked as a surveyor for the railroad, but the constant glare of the sun damaged his eyes, and he suffered eye problems for the rest of his life. This was compounded by a number of other health problems. George was ordained an apostle in 1903, at age thirty-three, and throughout the decade that followed he experienced extreme weakness, a sore back, frequent indigestion, and nervousness. Entries from his journal show the serious extent of his health problems: "My voice is so husky I can hardly speak. . . . My back is quite lame. . . . Had a bad spell with my stomach. . . . My heart seems to be weak this morning. . . . I am afraid I have overdone during the last year."[2]

Late in 1909, George's health collapsed, and the doctor ordered a complete year of rest. George Albert Smith, forty-two, was still on the slow road to recovery when he wrote the following letter to his friend and fellow apostle, Senator Reed Smoot, age fifty.

---

*George Albert's grandfather, George A. Smith (a first cousin to the Prophet Joseph Smith), and father, John Henry Smith, were both apostles and both served in the First Presidency of the Church.

Tucson, Arizona

April 9, 1912.

Senator Reed Smoot,

Washington, D. C.

My dear Reed:—

Your letter of last month was forwarded to me from Salt Lake City, and I was very pleased to get word from you again. I saw Albert Smith in Salt Lake City after I sent you word about him and I believe that he is making good.

I left home about the middle of March and spent the balance of the month in Los Angeles and Ocean Park, taking it easy and visiting friends. When I left home it was with the understanding that I would not return to the annual conference, but that I would take care of myself as best I could and build up my lost vigor. It seems a very slow process, but I presume that patience is the only means by which I may hope to be well again.

I have increased in weight since leaving home, having gained about four pounds, which, of course, is very gratifying to me, as I have steadily lost weight for the last year until I had lost thirteen pounds, so you will understand that to begin picking up again is somewhat encouraging.

I have never been discouraged for one moment and I fully believe that there is work for me to do yet, and that with the blessings of the Lord, I will find myself occupied, in the not far distant future, in the same pleasant work that it has been my privilege to enjoy during the past few years.

I most sincerely appreciate your great interest in me, and I thank you for it, and assure you that it is one of the pleasures of life to have as friend and brother such men as yourself.

Trusting that this will find you and yours enjoying the best that life affords, I remain

Yours affectionately,

Geo Albert Smith

P. S. I have come to Tucson for a couple of weeks as it is warm and pleasant.

———

Following his wife Lucy's advice to "rest, rest, rest," George slowly gained strength. Six months after writing the above letter, he spoke briefly at the October general conference, the first time he had spoken at conference in three years. The next year he traveled with other General Authorities to help dedicate a temple site in Cardston, Alberta, Canada. Then came a trip to Washington, D.C., and the first person he visited was Reed Smoot.

Although he suffered bouts of nervous exhaustion throughout the rest of his life, George Albert Smith served faithfully. In 1921, he and Lucy were called to England, where Elder Smith undertook the heavy responsibilities of president of the European Mission, successfully completing a two-year assignment despite tremendous problems brought about by World War I.

Although he lacked their robust physiques, George lived longer than either his father or grandfather. The prophecies made by Zebedee Coltrin in his 1884 patriarchal blessing to George were wonderfully fulfilled: George would become a "mighty apostle in the church and kingdom of God upon the earth, for none of thy father's family shall have more power with God than thou shalt have, for none shall excel thee. . . ." George would "remain upon the earth" until he was "satisfied with life."[3]

Ordained President of the Church on 21 May 1945 at age seventy-five, George Albert Smith lived his personal creed of being a friend to the friendless, visiting the sick and afflicted, loving people into doing the right thing, and not knowingly wounding the feelings of any. He had gained a special kind of strength. Shortly after World War II, when the Church was gathering relief supplies for Europe, President Smith toured a warehouse of goods, and, characteristic of his personal generosity, took off his own overcoat and placed it with a stack of items to be donated.

President Smith died on 4 April 1951, his eighty-first birthday. At his funeral, David O. McKay said he "lived as nearly as it is humanly possible for a man to live a Christ-like life."[4]

"Be Brave—and Patient"

During the first week of April 1916, Amy Brown Lyman, forty-four, then in the midst of her fifteen years of service as general secretary of the Relief Society, was apparently heavily involved in planning the annual Relief Society conference, which included six meetings, several musical numbers, and more than twenty speakers. Amy herself had been assigned to give the annual report of the Relief Society. Characteristically, Amy was also giving her time to social causes—1916 was the year she and Apostle George Albert Smith began working with Salt Lake City's Charity Organization Society.

Concerned about the pressure Amy was under, Susa Young Gates, the sixty-year-old editor of the *Relief Society Magazine,* penned the following undated letter on the back of a conference program—possibly in a pre-conference meeting since Susa, corresponding secretary of the Relief Society, was scheduled to speak in the same session as Amy. Susa would have been particularly sensitive to Amy's situation because she herself, involved in a flurry of missionary work, writing, publishing, and women's causes, had suffered a nervous and physical breakdown fifteen years earlier.

Amy dear—

God bless you and He will—Be comforted—You will feel better and stronger after this Conference than you have felt for many days. Your nerves will be quieted and sleep shall restore your vital forces.

Go on—there is a great work awaiting you. Be brave—and
patient—all will be well with you and yours—
Aunt Susa*

Susa Young Gates's mention of the great work awaiting Amy Brown
Lyman proved to be prophetic: Amy served as general secretary of the Relief
Society until 1928, when she was called as first counselor to Relief Society
President Louise Y. Robison. She served in that capacity until 1940, when she
was named as Relief Society president.

During these same years, Amy served as the first director of the Church
Social Welfare Department (1919–34); a member of the Utah legislature
(1923–24), where she helped pass legislation related to maternity, infant care,
and an institution for the mentally retarded; and a member of the board of
trustees for the American Fork Training School (1930–42). She also raised an
orphaned granddaughter; devoted countless hours to social work; and served
on the board of more than twenty-six local, national, and international
boards. Amy Brown Lyman, who was personally acquainted with every
general president of the Relief Society from Eliza R. Snow to Belle S. Spafford,
died in 1959, at age eighty-seven.

---

*The two women were not related; *aunt* was a term of endearment. In the same way, Amy referred
to Relief Society President Emmeline B. Wells as "Aunt Em."

"I Know That You Loved President Smith"

JULINA LAMBSON SMITH TO REED SMOOT
21 MARCH 1920

—

Julina Lambson Smith was the second of Joseph F. Smith's six wives. His first wife, Levira (daughter of Samuel H. Smith, first cousin to Joseph F.), obtained a divorce in 1867. Levira later visited Salt Lake City, and Julina recorded, "Some time later I was happily surprised to have a caller. Here was Levira. She said she was on her way through Salt Lake on her way East, but could not go without first seeing me and my baby. We again parted in sadness, but friendly, and my heart surely went out to her."[1]

Julina and Joseph had thirteen children, the seventh of whom was Joseph Fielding Smith. Julina was a trained midwife and served in the Relief Society general presidency as second counselor to Emmeline B. Wells from 1910 to 1921.

Joseph and Julina celebrated their fiftieth wedding anniversary on 5 May 1916. One photo shows them with more than fifty of their children and grandchildren. When President Smith died two and a half years later, on 19 November 1918, Reed Smoot made the following entry in his diary:

"I sent a telegram to Heber J. Grant as follows: 'Wire me date of President Smith's funeral. Have wired family through David.'* I received a telegram from Presidents Lund and Penrose as follows: 'President Smith died this morning four fifty oclock. No funeral.'† I sent the following telegram to Bp. David A. Smith: 'Evening papers announce the death of your father, President Smith. He was an ideal citizen, father, husband and servant of God. Please convey to

---

*David Asael Smith, Julina's son and younger brother to Joseph Fielding Smith. He was then serving as second counselor to Presiding Bishop Charles W. Nibley.

†Presidents Lund and Penrose later explained that Church leaders and the Smith family had decided that because of the influenza epidemic in the Salt Lake Valley, no public funeral services would be held.

the family the heartfelt sympathies of myself and my family. We sorrow with all Israel today. How we all loved and honored him. God bless his loved ones forever.' His death will be regretted by Mormon, Jew and Gentile. It will make a mighty change in the affairs of the church and Utah. I considered him my dearest friend on earth."[2]

A year and a half after the death of President Joseph F. Smith, his widow, seventy-one-year-old Julina, and his good friend and fellow apostle, fifty-eight-year-old Reed Smoot, exchanged the following letters.

Salt Lake City
March 21, 1920
Senator Reed Smoot
U.S. Senate, Washington D. C.
My Dear Brother Smoot:

I have wanted to write to you for a long time but felt backward as I generally have one of my children do my writing for me. I am such a poor correspondent, and seldom write to anyone yet I feel that I can write to you as I could to one of my own sons. I hope you will receive this in the spirit in which I say it.

I know that you loved President Smith and was always willing to receive council from him, because you knew that his counsel was right. I am in harmony with the Church and am trying to do what is right and follow counsel in all things. However, I have some views about political matters which I think I have a right to and feel that a person should be given the privilege of expressing honest conviction. I believe that President Smith always tried to take this view of things. I have felt to sympathize with you in some matters that have come before you for consideration in the senate, and have felt that you were entitled to your opinion and judgment being on the ground and fully acquainted with the situation far better than we at home could be. I have always felt that you would try to do the proper thing. In my own feelings I cannot endorse the course of President Wilson in all things and know of no good reason why I should, just because he is the President of the United States. I cannot feel that because of that fact his opinion should be superior in everything to all other men, and even if it is not, we are bound to follow his views because of his position. I will uphold and sustain him as the President, but claim the privilege to hold to my own opinion nevertheless, and [one] thing I am free to express is that I will be glad when we get a change in the White House, for anything would be an improvement, nothing could be worse.

Now, a few home words to you and Allie.* At the time of her mother's death,† I was not able to go out, so could not attend the funeral, nor could I attend that of her Aunt Eva's. Eva was a dear friend of mine, and a companion in our girlhood days. I remember going home with her to see the dear little baby Allie that was born in the Redfield home. Am I not right?

I have often thought of our trip to the Islands,‡ and felt that we should have another some day, but, alas, that thought has vanished.

I would like to visit Washington. I think I could help to cheer Allie,§ but it is not possible for me to come now. Some day I may. I want to thank you for your kindness to me. I have had tears at times when I think of it. I know you loved President Smith or you would not have been so kind to me in my sorrow. Some who,

---

*Reed Smoot's wife, Alpha May ("Allie") Eldredge Smoot.

†Allie's mother, Chloe Redfield Eldredge, had died a month and a half earlier, at age seventy-seven.

‡A trip to Hawaii in June of 1915, when President Smith dedicated the site for a temple in Laie. Reed Smoot said later of the dedicatory prayer: "Never in my life, did I hear such a prayer. The very ground seemed to be sacred, and he seemed as if he were talking face to face with the Father. I cannot and never will forget it if I live a thousand years." (Holzapfel and Shupe, 202.)

§Allie was frequently ill during this period.

before his death, manifested their spirit of love and goodwill, have now seemingly forgotten, and this makes me appreciate your kindness all the more.

May the Lord bless you and yours that you may live many years yet. The members of my family join me in these good wishes, for they all stand for Reed Smoot, for we know that he is performing a good work and is loyal to the right.

May you prosper and increase, is the prayer of your sister in the Gospel.

Julina L. Smith

"I Can Hardly Comprehend That He Is Gone"

April 6, 1920

Mrs. Julina L. Smith,

Care David A. Smith,

Bishop's Building,

Salt Lake City, Utah.

Dear Aunt Julina:*

Your letter, dated March 21, 1920, reached me day before yesterday, together with a letter from Donnette.† You will never know how much I appreciate the spirit of love and friendship manifested in your letter.

I loved President Smith more than any other man in this world, with perhaps the single exception of my father. In fact, I felt freer in talking to President Smith than I ever did with my father. The Lord never, in my opinion, created a better man nor one that tried to better serve him. I never expect to visit the President's office without memories of President Smith crowding my mind, and those memories shall always be laden with love and thanksgiving, for I shall never forget his friendship to me. Allie speaks of him so often, and I am quite sure that President Smith knew that Allie loved him as dearly as it was possible for her to do so. When President Smith died we felt a great loss, and sometimes I can hardly comprehend that he is gone.

---

*The two women were not related. *Aunt* was a term of endearment.

†Donnette Smith Kesler, Julina's daughter.

We would love to have you come and spend some time with us in Washington, and I want you to know that whenever you can do so, Allie and I will consider it a great favor if you will notify us and allow us to pay whatever expenses there may be in your coming and going. I want you to feel just as free to ask me for counsel or assistance as I would have been in asking President Smith. Please tell Donnette that we appreciate her kind letter of March 14.

Allie has been very poorly for the last three weeks, and in fact she has been in bed most of the time. At times it appears to me that she is losing a little of that determination to get well that she has been so blessed with, and whenever she has one of her severe attacks I imagine I can see that it is very much harder for her to recover, and at times she becomes almost discouraged. She joins me in asking our Heavenly Father's choicest blessings upon you and yours and all of the family of President Smith.

Your brother,

[Reed Smoot]

As Reed Smoot's biographer has noted, Allie Eldredge Smoot "contributed culture, charm, love, and domesticity, which produced a remarkable home life. . . . Through the entire marriage of forty-four years she was a devoted wife and mother, and provided the Apostle-Senator with a wonderful home atmosphere. . . . Smoot's political career was not only dependent on the monogamous character of his marriage relations, but in all probability it also was dependent on adherence to the most stringent standards of sexual morality. The Senator's personal integrity in these matters and the beauty, grace, and culture of Mrs. Smoot made certain that the most intensive prying and snooping went unrewarded."[3]

Allie Smoot's health continued to decline, and she was an invalid from 1920 until her death on 7 November 1928, at age sixty-five. Reed later married Alice Sheets, the mother-in-law of J. Willard Marriott.

Julina Lambson Smith lived for sixteen years after writing the above letter. She died on 10 January 1936, a week before her eighty-seventh birthday.

"I Do Most Fervently Appreciate Your Kind Words"

J. GOLDEN KIMBALL TO LEVI EDGAR YOUNG
7 JANUARY 1931

J. Golden Kimball was supposedly visiting a Church-owned woolen mill on assignment from the First Presidency. "He was wearing a long-tailed coat, which unfortunately got caught in a piece of machinery which proceeded to drag him around in a circular fashion. Unable to keep up with the rapid revolutions, he lost his balance and was swept wildly around the floor until the manager of the mill shut off the machine. Rushing to the dazed man's side, the manager shouted, 'Brother Kimball, speak to me! Speak to me!' Looking him straight in the eye, Golden retorted, 'I don't know why I should. I just passed you twelve times and you didn't speak to me once!'"[1]

The frequent repetition of such legends, even sixty years after Elder Kimball's death, is a tribute to his unpretentiousness, his goodwill, and his common sense. Many who hear these stories may be unaware that Jonathan Golden was the son of Heber C. Kimball and was born in Salt Lake City just six years after the Saints entered the Valley. Young Jonathan was barely fifteen when his father died. His mother, Christeen Kimball, later moved her family to Meadowville, near Bear Lake, Idaho.

"There was no house or improvement, and we commenced a fight for life," said J. Golden. "God knows it was a hard fight with poverty and terrible blizzards in winter. We felt some years that we had nine months winter and three months late fall. We worked, we toiled early and late, and the strange part of it was we never got discouraged. We hadn't sense enough to know when we had failed. Fifteen long years of hard work and sacrifice, but final success."[2]

Such reflections reveal the more serious side of J. Golden Kimball. Indeed, his biographer points out: "Despite his ten thousand friends, Brother Kimball was often a sad and lonely man. Much of his time was spent in meditation, much of it in sad reflection. How could this be, when he himself was the laugh-maker of the Church, when for decades men on the street have been calling for the latest J. Golden Kimball story, when audiences have listened for his pungent humor? Nevertheless, he was at heart a serious man. His wit was a natural but secondary bent. Agreeable to his calling, spiritual teaching was the great burden of his life's mission."[3]

The serious J. Golden Kimball was seventy-seven when he wrote the following letter to Levi Edgar Young, fifty-six. The two men had served together in the First Council of the Seventy for more than twenty years.

Salt Lake City
Jan 7th 1931
My dear friend and bro. Levi:
Your beautiful expression of brotherhood and true friendship helps one over the hill to the Kingdom of God just around the corner.

You are so courteous, kind and gentlemanly that I wonder oftentimes that you are not shocked at my crudness, but I feel sure that you and your race feel well toward me. I do most fervently appreciate your kind words of encouragement and the friendship of your family.

The Lord has blessed you in many ways and you are doing a noble work and His grace will be with you, for the Lord knows your desires and wishes and they will be realized.

Few men, if any, has more friends and you speak kind words of good cheer to the down and outer and I know of no greater gift.

Your words of cheer help me to "carry on" and prepare myself with faith, hope and good cheer to meet the inevitable and say in my heart, "Why fear death as its the greatest adventure of life."

God bless you and family and may you all live until you will
be glad to go somewhere for a change*—

Ever your bro. and friend
Golden

Known for his tolerance and compassion—as well as for his humor—
J. Golden Kimball served in the First Coucil of the Seventy from 1892 until
1938, when he died in an automobile accident near Reno, Nevada. He was
eighty-five at the time of his death.

---

*Levi Edgar Young lived a long, fruitful life, serving in the First Council of the Seventy for fifty-four
years before his death in 1963, at age eighty-nine.

Maori Serviceman Killed in Action

MATTHEW COWLEY TO THE ELKINGTON FAMILY
20 MAY 1943

The name of Matthew Cowley will be forever associated with the country of New Zealand, where he was affectionately known as *Tumuaki*, a term of endearment and respect that means "leader." Matthew's long friendship with New Zealanders began under difficult circumstances: he was only seventeen when he was called on his mission in 1914 and experiencing family problems. But the young elder took to the Maori culture and language with dedication and enthusiasm; at the end of his three-year mission he spoke Maori so fluently that President Joseph F. Smith asked him to remain in New Zealand to translate the Doctrine and Covenants and Pearl of Great Price into Maori, as well as revise the previous translation of the Book of Mormon.

Matthew returned home in 1919, studied law, and served as Senator Reed Smoot's executive secretary. He married Elva Eleanor Taylor in 1922; they had a daughter named Jewell. Matthew's law experience included two years as Salt Lake county attorney.

In 1938, forty-year-old Matthew Cowley was called as president of the New Zealand Mission. When he, Elva, and Jewell arrived in New Zealand, the members found that President Cowley was just as fluent as ever in Maori. Although American and Canadian missionaries in New Zealand had to return home in October of 1940 because of World War II, the Cowleys remained until the war ended in September of 1945. During his service to the Maori people, President Cowley experienced a number of miraculous healings, including the blessing of a blind boy who received his sight.

One of President Cowley's good friends in New Zealand was James Elkington, who had served a mission the same time Matthew served his first mission, and who was in a district presidency during President Cowley's tenure as mission president. Matthew Cowley was forty-five when he wrote the following letter to James Elkington and his family. He had just learned of the death of their son in the War.

—

May 20, 1943

Dear James, Hui Tau, and Family:

Yesterday morning when I read the name of H. Elkington in the list of those killed in action I knew that it must be Herbert, but I did not want to believe it until I had received a wire from you to verify it. I do not know when anything has stunned me so much as that. After being with you all at the *Hui* and then coming together on the boat so light-heartedly and happy, I did not realize that anything could happen so suddenly to change such happiness into tragic sorrow.

However we have no control over these things—man only proposes while God disposes—so there you are. We just have to accept the vicissitudes of life as they are meted out to us. After all the entire universe is groaning under the juggernaut of destruction which the wickedness of man is responsible for, so we all must bear our share of it.

The way things are going in the world today makes it more essential than ever that man shall have a hope for a continued existence after mortality. We have an assurance of this eternity of life, and in the loss of loved ones this alone gives us something to live for.

It is just a few weeks ago that I was talking to one of the Maori boys who had returned from the war. I asked him about Herbert, and he said that Herbert would either get killed or win the Victor's Cross. He said he was one of the most fearless men he had ever seen and was always the first to expose himself to the greatest danger. He also said, as I remember, that Herbert was the best dispatch rider in the New Zealand forces. Anyone who knew Herbert would know that he would be just that kind of soldier. And the same could be said of Sam. They were twins both physically and spiritually. There was no limit to their energy.*

When I was visiting at the home of Brother Going before he died, he told me that Sam and Herbert were the two best missionaries that had ever been to his home. I asked him why he thought that and he replied that they had the most spirited souls he had ever seen. Brother Going liked people who were always busy, and so naturally the twins were attractive to him.

I felt sorry when the twins did not go away together but now I feel that it was for the best that Sam has been kept behind. He will feel that part of his own life has been taken, but at the same time Herbert will be kept alive in him, and this should be a great incentive for him to do great things in life for both of them. Sam will be a great leader among his people if his energy is controlled and his course in life is directed by the priesthood. Whatever happens he must not let Herbert down by taking the course of least resistance. For that matter none of us must let him down.

He has made the supreme sacrifice for all of us. He died that the freedom we have known might be continued unto us; that we might have a more abundant life. We can only honor a sacrifice such as that by doing bigger and better things in life. Surely our boys are not dying so that their people may degenerate to immorality. If they are dying for anything it is to give us a moral uplift; to urge us to make the world a better place in which to live. If we do not live for the virtues on the home front, of what value is this great sacrifice of human lives on the battlefields? Why fight for freedom if we are going to become slaves to our

*Sam was Herbert's twin brother who also served in the War. He survived.

baser selves? Our love for Herbert, Arthur, and the others means more to us than that.

James and Hui Tau, there is little that I can say to give you comfort in such a time as this. Time will heal the wound and bring him back to you. He is separated from you for a season, but you cannot lose him. The sealing power of the priesthood will make him yours forever, worlds without end. You have been blessed with a large family, and now God has only exacted a tithe of what he has given you. God expected much of you when he blessed your home with so many children, and you have failed neither God nor your children.

Hui Tau, you especially have been blessed. You have not been too strong physically, but you have borne your children and everyone of them has come with a sound constitution. It is not a usual thing for a mother who suffered as you to give birth to children, and so many of them, who have no nervous nor physical disorders.

You and James have both had wonderful parents, and it must be a joy to you both to know that your children have had just as good parents as you had. To me this would be a reward greater than I deserve.

The *Hui* at Nelson was one of the best I have ever attended; there was such a beautiful spirit, and the family reunion around the old folks fairly thrilled me. The picture of it all will remain in mind and inspire me as long as I live. Your Primary demonstration was charming, and the tribute James paid to his parents and to his wife while speaking touched everyone. Of course he said only what all the children would have said, but then he was the proper one to say it.

None of us realized what sorrow would follow so soon that occasion of rejoicing, but then although we did not know about

Herbert at the time, we will always associate our beautiful *Hui* with the passing of a beautiful life. We will always remember now these two events in connection with each other.

Sister Cowley and Jewell join me in sending love, blessings, and sympathy in this great sorrow which has come to you. I wish I could be with you in person; *kei kona hoki taku wairua.*

Sincerely your brother,
Matthew Cowley

In October of 1945, three weeks after the Cowleys returned from New Zealand, Matthew was called to the Quorum of the Twelve. The next year he suffered a heart attack while addressing a group of students at Brigham Young University. He recovered, however, and subsequently served as president of the Pacific Mission—an area that included the New Zealand, Australia, Tahiti, Tonga, Samoa, Central Pacific, and Hawaii missions. This calling allowed Elder and Sister Cowley to visit their beloved New Zealand a number of times. Their adopted son, Duncan Meha Cowley (born in 1939), was a native of New Zealand.

In December of 1953, Brother and Sister Cowley traveled to California with President McKay and several others to attend the cornerstone laying ceremonies for the Los Angeles Temple. The ceremonies took place on Friday, 11 December. The next day, when President McKay saw the Cowleys, Elder Cowley mentioned that he wasn't feeling well. He and Elva visited Matthew's brother Joseph that evening, and as they were leaving, Joe said, "Now, Matt take care of yourself. We want you with us a long, long time." Elder Cowley said, "Joe, life is eternal." The next morning, around 4:45 A.M., Matthew Cowley, age fifty-six, died quietly in his sleep.[1]

"Your Father Was a Truly Wonderful Man"

BELLE S. SPAFFORD TO ETHEL TAYLOR SESSIONS
16 NOVEMBER 1950

⌐

Marion Isabelle ("Belle") Sims Smith Spafford and Ethel Taylor Sessions formed a lifelong friendship when they were young. Belle's letters to Ethel, now preserved in the L. Tom Perry Special Collections Library at Brigham Young University, cover more than forty years.

Belle Smith studied social work at the University of Utah and Brigham Young University; she also taught retarded children at BYU's Training School. After her marriage to Willis Earl Spafford in 1921, she returned to BYU to develop special classes for children. She was called to the Relief Society general board in 1935 and as a counselor to Relief Society President Amy Brown Lyman in 1942. She became general president of the Relief Society in 1945, at age forty-nine.

Ethel's father, Thomas Nicholls Taylor, was a prominent Church leader and businessman in Provo, Utah. He founded Taylor Brothers Company and was the president of Provo Building and Loan. He also served as bishop of the Provo Third Ward and was called as president of the Utah Stake in 1919. When he died in 1950, at age eighty-two, Ethel received the following letter from Belle. (Belle's own father, John Gibson Smith, died before Belle was born.)

⌐

November 16, 1950
Mrs. Ethel Sessions
841 South Serreno Street
Los Angeles, California

Dear Ethel:

Florence Madsen* and I were in the East conducting Relief Society conventions when we learned of the death of your dear father. I would have written you immediately but did not have my address book with me.[†]

Ethel, I know your father's death has been a very difficult experience for you. I know of few daughters so devoted to a father, or few fathers to whom a daughter meant so much. He relied upon you in so many ways and, to my knowledge, you never failed him in anything. What a comfort your many years of intimate and loving companionship must be to you now.

Your father was a truly wonderful man, big in all that he did. He was a builder of both Church and community and has won and held the respect of everyone. My brother, John,[‡] thought there was no one in Provo to equal him. He has passed on to his family a truly good name, which Ecclesiastes tells us is "Better than precious ointment."[§]

What a blessing is our knowledge of the gospel at times like this. How happy your father must be to be reunited with your dear mother.[**]

Ethel, please accept my deepest sympathy. I know that no matter how long we expect death it is always a shock and a deep sorrow to lose someone we love. May the choice blessings of our

---

*Florence Jepperson Madsen was a prominent musician and member of the Relief Society general board. She was well known for conducting Relief Society choirs.

[†]Ethel's father had died on 24 October.

[‡]Belle's brother John Sims Smith had died in 1924 at the age of forty-one.

[§]Ecclesiastes 7:1: "A good name is better than precious ointment; and the day of death than the day of one's birth."

[**]Ethel's mother, Maud Rogers Taylor, had died in 1942 at the age of seventy.

Heavenly Father be with you to comfort you and may you take comfort in the joy you have always brought into the life of your father.

Affectionately,

Belle S. Spafford

Belle's letters to Ethel cover a virtual lifetime; through them one can trace the histories of both women. Belle suffered her own sorrows when her husband and daughter both died within a year and a half: her husband, Willis, on 26 January 1963, at age seventy-one; and her daughter, Mary Spafford Kemp, on 28 March 1964, at age forty.

Belle apparently wrote her last letter to Ethel in 1980, when they were both in their eighties.

Belle S. Spafford served as president of the Relief Society for twenty-nine and a half years, longer than any other woman. When she was called at the end of World War II, there were approximately 100,000 members of the Relief Society, most of them in the western United States. When she was released in 1974, Relief Society membership numbered close to one million, with sisters in sixty-five different countries. (She also served as president of the National Council of Women for two years.)

At her release, President Kimball said: "Sister Spafford has been a strong and vibrant voice in many lands and many countries and among many peoples. Her voice has been heard in many places where it required insight and courage and forthrightness to stand almost alone against sometimes strange ideologies. She is a woman of education, refinement, and a leader in thought and action. She has considerable secular and spiritual training. She has honorary degrees from two great universities. She has been active in women's organizations, national and international, and has traveled abroad in her special work. Her late husband, Willis Earl Spafford, and her children sustained her in her monumental labors. She has traveled widely, written much, and spoken to numerous groups of people in many lands. . . . She is distinguished, honored, and loved."[1]

"I Fairly Shouted for Joy"

HUGH B. BROWN TO ADAM S. BENNION

7 APRIL 1953

—

In the spring of 1950, Hugh B. Brown, who had previously served as a mission president, a stake president, and coordinator for LDS servicemen, received an offer to leave his teaching post at Brigham Young University and become general counsel for an oil company in Alberta, Canada. After consulting with the First Presidency, he accepted the well-paying job and became a manager as well as general counsel. He earned more than twenty times his salary the first year—$100,000 compared to his annual salary at BYU of $4,500.

Hugh's work took him into the Rocky Mountains, where he supervised oil-drilling operations. In 1953 he was sixty-nine years old and apparently nearing retirement when he wrote the following letter to Adam S. Bennion, sixty-six.

—

April 7, 1953
Dr. Adam S. Bennion
47 E. South Temple Street
Salt Lake City, Utah
Dear Brother Bennion:
At ten o'clock yesterday morning I was far back in the Canadian Rockies, six thousand feet above sea level, in a camp where we are drilling for oil. During Sunday I was able to get part of the Conference on a small battery radio set, but on Monday the signals were very indistinct. However, imagine my joy when, with the radio pressed against my ear, I heard the voice of

106

President Clark as he presented the names of the General Authorities of the Church; and when your name was mentioned as the new Apostle I fairly shouted for joy.*

I know you will have thousands of letters and telegrams and that you will, of course, be unable to answer all of them. May I just say here that this letter needs no answer, but I cannot refrain from writing to extend my congratulations and assure you of my support. Zina[†] shares my feeling in that a better choice could not have been made.

Ever since I first met you at the B.Y.U. Summer School in 1919[‡] I have felt that your place was among the general authorities of the Church, and each time there has been a vacancy I have secretly nominated you for the position. You will have the love and confidence, admiration and support of all of the Church. With the blessings of our heavenly Father, and with your unusual training and background, you will add to your already enviable record as a special messenger to the youth of the Church.

I have always believed that the decisions of the First Presidency are prompted by the inspiration and revelation of the Lord. That faith has been strengthened by your appointment.

Zina joins in extending love and blessings to you and Minerva.[§]

Cordially and faithfully yours,

Hugh

HBB:B

---

*Elder Bennion filled the vacancy created by John A. Widtsoe's death.

[†]Zina Card Brown. She and Hugh were married on 17 June 1908.

[‡]The actual year was 1920. (Campbell and Poll, 95.)

[§]Minerva Young Bennion. She and Adam were married on 14 September 1911.

⸺

In his memoirs, Hugh B. Brown recorded what happened six months after he wrote this letter: "I was up in the Canadian Rockies, supervising the drilling of an oil well. Although my family was in good health and good spirits and I was making good money, more than ever before, I was deeply depressed and worried and could not understand why. Early one morning I went up into the mountains and talked with the Lord in prayer. I said to him, 'It is apparent that I am going to become a millionaire. I pray thee, O Lord, not to let it happen if it will be detrimental to me or to my family.'"

The next night a phone call came from Salt Lake City: "This is David O. McKay calling. The Lord wants you to spend the balance of your life in the service of the Church."[1] Hugh B. Brown thus became an Assistant to the Twelve in October of 1953, and he and Adam S. Bennion served as fellow General Authorities for four years.

In life, and in death, a unique bond existed between Hugh and Adam. They shared an interest in education, a love of literature, and a special feeling for the youth of the Church. When Elder Bennion died, on 11 February 1958, at age seventy-one, the man chosen to fill the vacancy in the Twelve was Hugh B. Brown. "This calling was very humbling indeed," Elder Brown wrote in his journal, "but it is in fulfillment of a life-long ambition of my beloved mother, who predicted it when I was but a boy."[2]

Hugh B. Brown served for another seventeen years, including most of the turbulent 1960s as a counselor to David O. McKay. Hugh B. Brown died in the winter of 1975, when he was ninety-two. It was 2 December, the eighty-ninth anniversary of his friend Adam S. Bennion's birth.*

---

*Elder ElRay L. Christiansen, an Assistant to the Twelve, died the same day. It was the first time since the deaths of Joseph and Hyrum Smith, in 1844, that two General Authorities had died on the same day.

"Dr. Martin . . . Prescribed Immediate Surgery"

In the spring of 1950—just six and a half years after his call to the Quorum of the Twelve—Spencer W. Kimball began experiencing problems with his throat. He found himself frequently hoarse, though he had no cough or congestion. When a doctor found a white spot on one of Spencer's vocal cords, Elder Kimball confided to his journal: "Cancer! Cancer of the throat would render me useless from now on to the Church."[1] Only fifteen months earlier, Spencer's younger sister Helen Kimball Farr had died of cancer at age forty-seven, and he had feared cancer ever since. A biopsy revealed no cancer, however, and even a recommended cauterization was not necessary after he received a blessing.

Around Christmas of 1956, the problem recurred. Three months later, Spencer visited a specialist in New York City, who performed a biopsy and instructed Spencer not to use his voice for thirty days. Spencer complied, and while the biopsy was inconclusive, his throat did not heal as expected. Despite this burden, he attempted to carry on his Church responsibilities with a whisper or with no voice at all. By July he was facing a radical operation that meant the complete removal of one vocal cord and part of the other. Shortly after the operation, Spencer, sixty-two, wrote the following letter to longtime friend, fellow Arizonan, and associate in the Quorum of the Twelve, Delbert L. Stapley, sixty.

New York City, New York
Aug 4 1957
Dear Del,
Your letter was most welcome as was your phone call and we

appreciate more than we express your thoughtful consideration. We were shocked to learn of the rather sudden passing of our brother-in-law, Bernard Williams. In the same mail we had word from the family at Mesa [Arizona]. A little surprised also about Al Clayton. We have expected it so long and it seemed from outward appearances that he was not so much worse than the last time we saw him—I rather expected he might last for weeks. Glad you could be there to speak and comfort Erma and the family. Erma has been the soul of loyalty and devotion to him.

We have had two hectic weeks since seeing you. Since I did not get to talk to you much about it, you might be interested in some details: I worried much for two months over the urgency Dr. Cowan seemed to assign to the trip to New York to let Dr. Martin "take another look at it." Though he would not commit himself much about it, the fact which he emphasized that the wound was not healing was ominous. That nearly always means trouble and trouble it really was.

I was disturbed and conscience smitten somewhat when I came back in March without having considered it fully with the Brethren but as you probably know I felt at that time it would be little or nothing more than a biopsy and judging by my 1950 biopsy I had little fear of being incapacitated or losing my voice since nothing of that kind happened then. When in March I once got on the assembly line there seemed to be no place to get off and almost before I knew what was going on I had partially lost my voice and was silenced for the past five months.

I wondered if the Brethren, particularly the Presidency, wondered about such summary action without consulting them. At any rate, I made up my mind that I would not move again without counsel. I belong to the Church, body, mind and soul, and I realize that I had no right to take any action on my own volition which could impair my service to the Church. Accordingly, I sought and obtained an interview with President McKay.

Since his hearing is slightly impaired and my voice off so much, it seemed best to present myself in writing. My letter expressed my surprise at the speed and the outcome of the first encounter with the doctors and hospital here and the President said "he had wondered." He suggested that I return the next day to give him time to meditate and pray about the matter, and in that second visit he said, "I have prayed about this and considered it and believe that what I am going to advise is correct." He then said if I wanted to depend wholly on faith that they would all join with me but that he felt the Lord expected us to use the skill which He has given man and to go as far toward solving our own problems as we could, then depend on Him to place His blessing upon it and complete it. He spoke of Helen Keller and what she had done with so many handicaps and I felt that he feared the operation necessary. I had been hoping against hope that he would FEEL an optimism that the operation might be bypassed. I told Pres. McKay I would follow his advice. I was going to ask him to give me a blessing but he was gone to California when I was ready to ask for it. I went to Pres. Clark who gave me a wonderful blessing but from what he said I had the impression that he felt there was little chance to avoid the devastating surgery which would take my voice so finally. Much in his prayer was for the ability to adjust to conditions. He also felt I should come to N. Y. and to follow the advice and counsel of Dr. Cowan and Dr. Martin. Consequently, I had my <u>mind</u> made up to go to surgery or whatever was properly recommended as much as I recoiled at the thought of the finality of such. Dr. Cowan had been so late in calling Dr. Hayes Martin that he found him leaving for vacation but he made an appointment for Dr. Martin to give my throat another look on July 26th before leaving for his vacation.

We hurriedly made arrangements, cancelled appointments and left Tuesday July 23rd via Union Pacific with destination known, but destiny unknown. We assumed that Dr. Martin would look it over, make recommendations, and that we would either wait around through his vacation or go back hom[e] and return later. Hence we were somewhat unprepared for what we found.

Our trip East was uneventful except we stopped over 24 hours in Ann Arbor, Michigan, and thoroughly enjoyed every minute of it with our son, LeVan, and his family. We visited the grave of our son, Andrew's, little girl who died there, and we then came on to New York and were met by Brother and Sister Harold B. Lee who went with us to the doctors' office and he stood in with us through the interview.

Dr. Martin quickly sized up the situation and prescribed immediate surgery. He seemed not to dare to leave it till Sept. after his vacation since it was definitely infected. He postponed his leaving and placed me ahead of other patients and set Monday 29th for surgery. This was a time when I was everlastingly grateful for the presence and strength of Bro. Lee. One entire cord was to be removed and part of the other with the certain loss of much of my power of speech. It helped in the decision to have him nod approval.

Camilla was quite unprepared for the shock. This was Friday. I was to enter the hospital Sunday. I had made up my <u>mind</u> to it but I found my spirit fighting it. All through Friday, Saturday and Sunday morning I was fighting a mighty battle inside. The idea was stifling, terror-ridden. We came in March to what we assumed would be a simple operation and returned to 5 months near silence but always with HOPE of return of voice. I had anticipated a month or two of voice rest, then to have my voice back. As the months piled up two, three, four, five, I came to realize I had been holding on to little more than soap bubbles in the air. This time there was no promise, not even a hope that I could converse. It was devastatingly final and though I gave my consent and knew before leaving the Brethren and Salt Lake City that I would, yet my soul still rebelled through the hours of those two days.

Pres. and Sister Stan McAllister took us all to dinner Friday night—the Ken Dyers just returning from West German Mission Presidency, the Mortimers, the Lees and the Kimballs. I talked— I used my voice—I expended it. I had developed a fair volume above the whisper which I had saved as directed by Dr. Cowan— saved as a miser saves his coins, but Monday it would all be cut out, taken from me forever. I'd use it and enjoy it. It had come to give promise of a fairly usable voice but one more day, and gone for good, so with no opposition from the doctor I used it. How good it seemed to be able to speak even so poorly but above a whisper.

Saturday morning Andrew, our son, came down from Schenectady and we celebrated. All day together, the three of us. Around the island, over to Staten Island, to some good shows. How wonderful to have our sweet boy with us, but all the time I was battling with myself. Andrew still was counselor in Westchester Ward (they were replacing him this Sunday) so we went out on the train to the ward, his ward. It rained hard while we were there. Then we came back to the city and to the Memorial Hospital. He and Camilla took me to task, argued with me, [pled] with me and finally I capitulated. I gave up and quit fighting. My mind had been made up, now my spirit yielded and my body relaxed and I was ready.

Brother Lee and Bro. Fugal came in Monday morning and

administered to me and I felt at peace—no fear, no resistance. Brother Lee was good enough to return and stand by with Camilla during the operation.

The moment came for the double injection. And when I was awake again it would be gone! Up the hall on the truck, up the elevator and to the surgery room. I wanted a look at that room since it was going to cost so much for its use for the next little while. Lights, and instruments, and nurses with covered hair and mouth and now the doctors. I said to the young doctor: "Just to satisfy my curiosity what are you doing on the rim of my face?" They don't give you much satisfaction—it is really none of your business, you know—you are only the patient—but from what he said and what I could still feel, the young surgeon was preparing the way for Dr. Martin. From my ears to my chin end, he was putting a needle through with thread or string or rope or cable?? to which to attach the soaker towels so they would not get moved out of place during the operation. The several bruised places on my neck and chest may have come later, I didn't feel them but it seemed they must have nailed down the towels and tied back the flaps of flesh to these anchors after they had made the large incision from my chin down my throat. I was gone—I didn't feel the final cut but I remember as I lost consciousness, "Is that you, Dr. Martin?" and after his acquiescence, "There are thousands of people praying for you this morning that you will be blessed in your decisions." Then I gave up.

I was in the recovery pavilion only 4 or 5 hours this time instead of the 18 or 20 hours before, in March. They had given me less dosage, perhaps more local anaesthetic, and I came out of it more easily. And when they wheeled me back to my room, what a sight I was! The tube in my windpipe made me wheeze like an old worn out horse. All the air coming through the tube left me none for speech. I could gasp only one word or even a syllable with one breath. I felt fairly good when Brother Lee left to catch the train for Palmyra, better in fact than I have felt since. I still had a little fringe of voice way down in the lower register and I had great hope that I could take of that little and make something of it, but the next day it was gone totally, so I am back now to soft, almost unintelligible whisper and mighty grateful to be able to whisper.

Those were hectic days in the hospital, six of them with almost no sleep, much pain in my neck and chest, a dull headache constantly and a very sore throat which felt like a strep throat.

Perhaps I have gone into more details than necessary but you and I have always been quite confidential regarding our heart pains, our bellyaches, our finances, our mutual friends and acquaintances and since you were in Arizona and I could not talk it through with you, I wondered if you might like to just visit (via typewriter) a little. . . . I have been keeping [the incision] hidden. This morning (Monday Aug 5) the doctor said to leave it open except when out in the streets.

Those were difficult days in the hospital, sleepless ones with considerable pain which was constant. Camilla spent the days with me. It was the never ending nights that tried my soul.

Pres. McAllister and Pres. Payne of the Stake Presidency called and gave me a blessing. Pres. McAllister and wife who live nearer came again more than once and brought roses. Brother Lee and wife left us a beautiful bouquet which lasted all week and the very lovely bouquet from you brethren came mid-week and is still with us and most beautiful.

We went to Manhattan Ward for Sunday School and Testimony Meeting yesterday, though I was not so pious as it might seem. My troubles seemed to hurt [less] where something is going on than in bed where I have nothing else to do but think of my troubles. We returned to the evening meeting with my neck fully bundled up.

While my pain has been so intense I have given less thought to the bleak future. Now that the wounds are healing, my mind is not wholly on sore throats and chest discolorations.

Though the doctors have given no indication when we may leave "their embrace," we hope it will not be more than another week or 10 days before we can start home.

Hope that you are taking care of yourself; that Ethel is feeling good; that the work at the office is not too burdensome, and give our love to any interested folks.

Camilla joins me in kindest wishes, and affection.

Spencer W. Kimball

To: Elder Delbert L. Stapley
Salt Lake City

Four weeks after the operation, Spencer and Camilla were finally able to return home to Utah. Once again, however, Spencer was forced to carry on without using his voice, now drastically weakened by the operation. (Spencer thus spent most of the year of 1957 in silence.) In November, three months after the operation, Spencer's throat was pronounced healed. A month later he attended a stake conference in the Gila Valley in Arizona with his friend Delbert L. Stapley.

Spencer, who had not spoken at a conference since his operation, was offered the chance to speak by Elder Stapley. "[He] decided that if ever he were to speak in public again he would have to brave a first time and there would be no more sympathetic group in the whole Church for him than this one. He started by telling the congregation that he had gone to New York and fallen among cutthroats and thieves who had slit his throat and stolen his voice. The audience laughed heartily and both he and they relaxed. He was home, he was back at his work again."[2]

A tireless worker, Spencer W. Kimball traveled and spoke widely throughout the 1960s. At the end of 1973, following the death of President Harold B. Lee—who had been such a good friend to the Kimballs—Elder Kimball was ordained the twelfth President of the Church, at age seventy-eight. He served in that capacity until his death in 1985, a remarkable period in Church history. Millions grew to love his distinct, moving, prophetic voice.

"I Was Very Happy to Hear Your Name Read"

J. WILLARD MARRIOTT TO GORDON B. HINCKLEY
29 APRIL 1958

On Saturday evening, 5 April 1958, Gordon B. Hinckley, then serving as president of the East Millcreek Stake in Salt Lake City, received a phone call from David O. McKay. The Church president asked if Gordon could come to his office. "After greeting him cordially, President McKay got right to the point: He wished for Gordon to accept a call to serve as an Assistant to the Twelve.

"President McKay's words shocked Gordon. 'It was a blow, a complete surprise,' he admitted. 'I had worked around the Church administration building* for many years, and I knew these men who were called as General Authorities very well. I knew their strengths and their weaknesses. I knew they were special people, and to join their ranks was an almost unbelievable thing. It was overwhelming to have the President of the Church issue such a call.'"[1]

Elder Hinckley, forty-seven, was sustained the next day, 6 April, at general conference. Three weeks later he received the following letter from prominent LDS businessman and philanthropist J. Willard Marriott, fifty-seven. Brother Marriott had previously served as president of the Washington, D.C. Stake.

April 29, 1958
Dear Gordon:
I was very happy to hear your name read at the recent

---

*Gordon B. Hinckley had worked full time for the Church for nearly forty years. In 1951 he became executive secretary of the General Missionary Committee.

conference. With your vast experience in Church work, I am sure you are going to be an excellent asset to the Twelve.

I hope you will have continued success, health and strength. I know you will have the love and cooperation of all the members of the Church with whom you are associated.

> With best personal regards, I am
> Sincerely,
> J. Willard Marriott

Mr. Gordon B. Hinckley
Church Office Building
47 East South Temple Street
Salt Lake City, Utah

Elder Hinckley was called to the Quorum of the Twelve in September of 1961, and his friendship with the Marriott family continued throughout the years. In April of 1980, twenty-two years after the preceding letter was written, Elder Hinckley and J. Willard Marriott's son (J. Willard Marriott Jr.), appeared together on the *Today* show, where they were interviewed by Tom Brokaw. When asked to identify the key to the Church's growth, Elder Hinckley said, "It meets the spiritual and social needs of members and gives motivation to their lives. It is an anchor of sorts in an uncertain world."[2]

"Your Warm and Friendly Presence"

G. HOMER DURHAM TO THOMAS S. MONSON
30 JUNE 1976

Thomas S. Monson was a young student at the University of Utah in the late 1940s when he took a history class from G. Homer Durham. Brother Durham, who had been a missionary companion of Gordon B. Hinckley in England, had already written a biography of Joseph Smith and was a contributing editor for the *Improvement Era*. He was appointed president of Arizona State University in 1960, a post he held for nine years. In 1969, six years after Thomas S. Monson was called to the Quorum of the Twelve, Homer became Utah's first commissioner of higher education. This brought him into frequent contact with Elder Monson, then serving on the Utah State Board of Regents.

In March of 1976, at the age of sixty-five, G. Homer Durham was called as a regional representative. He wrote the following letter after accepting a research professorship at the University of Utah a few months later. Elder Monson was forty-eight.

June 30, 1976
Elder Thomas S. Monson   PERSONAL
Utah State Board of Regents
50 East North Temple Street
Salt Lake City, Utah 84150
Dear Tom:

As I vacate the office of the Utah Commissioner of Higher Education, I wish to acknowledge to you personally how much I have appreciated the kindness, support, and intelligent oversight you have provided me.

As you know, I was largely persuaded to leave the presidency of Arizona State University by our dear friend and brother, Richard L. Evans. In many telephone calls back and forth, accompanied by much earnest thought and prayer, we came to the decision that this was what Eudora* and I were supposed to do at that time. His sustaining influence, followed by that of President Harold B. Lee during the critical hours of our Supreme Court case, followed by your warm and friendly presence on the Board, together with your vigorous leadership and perception, have meant more to me than I can ever say.

When, in January, 1973, you were the instrumentality through which I was called to the presidency of the Salt Lake Central Stake, that opportunity for service, accompanied by the renewal of the executive leadership to which I had become accustomed (and somewhat thwarted by the complex nature of our Utah System!), has been the greatest blessing of the past seven years, together with its consequences.

Please know of my eternal gratitude and my deep appreciation for the great and similar service you have performed on so many, many fronts.

Sincerely yours,
Homer
G. Homer Durham
Commissioner of Higher Education
And Chief Executive Officer

Less than a year after writing this letter, G. Homer Durham was called to the First Quorum of the Seventy. Four years after that, in October of 1981, he

---

*Eudora Widtsoe Durham, daughter of Apostle John A. Widtsoe and Leah Dunford Widtsoe. She and G. Homer Durham were married on 20 June 1936.

was ordained to the Presidency of the First Quorum of the Seventy—even though he was recovering from open-heart surgery at the time.

Elder Durham, the author of many important historical works himself, served as managing director of the Church historical department. He also combined talents with his former missionary companion, President Hinckley, in writing the hymn "My Redeemer Lives," with President Hinckley writing the text and Elder Durham composing the music.

G. Homer Durham died of a heart attack on 10 January 1985, at the age of seventy-three. When President Monson spoke on gratitude in the April 1992 general conference, he paid tribute to his longtime friend:

"May I express public gratitude for three of my own teachers. I thank G. Homer Durham, my history professor. He taught the truth, 'The past is behind; learn from it.' He loved his subject; he loved his students. The love in his classroom opened the windows of my mind, that learning might enter."[1]

Part 4

~

"ANXIOUSLY ENGAGED"

THE WORK OF
THE KINGDOM

"Day after Day I Continued . . . to Write"

OLIVER COWDERY TO W. W. PHELPS
7 SEPTEMBER 1834

Born in New Jersey in 1792, William Wines [W. W.] Phelps began working as a newspaper editor in New York in the early 1820s. Around 1828 he began publishing an anti-Masonic newspaper called the *Ontario Phoenix*. During 1830 he obtained a copy of the Book of Mormon, and in December of that year he met Joseph Smith for the first time.

Just a few weeks after meeting the Prophet, William received a letter from anti-Mormon newspaper publisher E. D. Howe inquiring about Mormonism. Thinking Phelps to be "an avowed infidel," Howe was surprised at William's response: "To be sure, I am acquainted with a number of the persons concerned in the publication, called the 'Book of Mormon.'—Joseph Smith is a person of very limited abilities in common learning—but his knowledge of *divine things*, since the appearance of his book, has astonished many. Mr. [Martin] Harris . . . is honest, and sincerely declares upon his soul's salvation that the book is true, and was interpreted by Joseph Smith, through a pair of silver spectacles, found with the plates."[1]

Within months, though they had not yet been baptized, W. W. Phelps and his family joined the Saints in Kirtland, Ohio. Section 55 of the Doctrine and Covenants, received in June of 1831, instructed William to assist Oliver Cowdery in the "work of printing, and of selecting and writing books for schools in this church" (D&C 55:4). William thus began a distinguished writing and editing career in the service of the Church. In 1834, Oliver Cowdery, twenty-seven, wrote eight letters to W. W. Phelps, forty-two, that detailed the history of the Restoration. The following is one of these letters:

Norton, Medina co. Ohio, Sabbath evening, September 7, 1834.

DEAR BROTHER,

Before leaving home, I promised, if I tarried long, to write; and while a few moments are now allowed me for reflection, aside from the cares and common conversation of my friends in this place, I have thought that were I to communicate them to you, might, perhaps, if they should not prove especially beneficial to yourself, by confirming you in the faith of the gospel, at least be interesting, since it has pleased our heavenly Father to call us both to rejoice in the same hope of eternal life. And by giving them publicity, some thousands who have embraced the same covenant, may learn something more particular upon the rise of this church, in this last time. And while the gray evening is fast changing into a settled darkness, my heart responds with the happy millions who are in the presence of the Lamb, and are past the power of temptation, in rendering thanks, though feebly, to the same Parent. . . .

Near the time of the setting of the Sun, Sabbath evening, April 5th, 1829, my natural eyes, for the first time beheld this brother [Joseph Smith]. He then resided in Harmony, Susquehanna county Penn. On Monday the 6th, I assisted him in arranging some business of a temporal nature, and on Tuesday the 7th, commenced to write the book of Mormon. These were days never to be forgotten—to sit under the sound of a voice dictated by the inspiration of heaven, awakened the utmost gratitude of this bosom! Day after day I continued, uninterrupted, to write from his mouth, as he translated, with the Urim and Thummim, or, as the Nephites would have said, "Interpreters," the history, or record, called "The book of Mormon."

To notice, in even few words, the interesting account given

126

by Mormon, and his faithful son Moroni, of a people once beloved and favored of heaven, would supersede my present design: I shall therefore defer this to a future period, and as I said in the introduction, I shall . . . pass more directly to some few incidents immediately connected with the rise of this church, which may be entertaining to some thousands who have stepped forward, amid the frowns of bigots and the calumny of hypocrites, and embraced the gospel of Christ.

No men in their sober senses, could translate and write the directions given to the Nephites, from the mouth of the Savior, of the precise manner in which men should build up his church, and especially, when corruption had spread an uncertainty over all forms and systems practiced among men, without desiring a privilege of showing the willingness of the heart by being buried in the liquid grave, to answer a "good conscience by the resurrection of Jesus Christ."

After writing the account given of the Savior's ministry to the remnant of the seed of Jacob, upon this continent, it was easily to be seen, as the prophet said would be, that darkness covered the earth and gross darkness the minds of the people. On reflecting further, it was as easily to be seen, that amid the great strife and noise concerning religion, none had authority from God to administer the ordinances of the gospel. For, the question might be asked, have men authority to administer in the name of Christ, who deny revelations? when his testimony is no less than the spirit of prophecy? and his religion based, built, and sustained by immediate revelations in all ages of the world, when he has had a people on earth? If these facts were buried, and carefully concealed by men whose craft would have been in danger, if once permitted to shine in the faces of men, they were no longer to us;

and we only waited for the commandment to be given, "Arise and be baptized."

This was not long desired before it was realized. The Lord, who is rich in mercy, and ever willing to answer the consistent prayer of the humble, after we had called upon him in a fervent manner, aside from the abodes of men, condescended to manifest to us his will. On a sudden, as from the midst of eternity, the voice of the Redeemer spake peace to us, while the veil was parted and the angel of God* came down clothed with glory, and delivered the anxiously looked for message, and the keys of the gospel of repentance!—What joy! what wonder! what amazement! While the world were racked and distracted—while millions were [groping] as the blind for the wall, and while all men were resting upon uncertainty, as a general mass, our eyes beheld—our ears heard. As in the "blaze of day;" yes, more— above the glitter of the May† Sun beam, which then shed its brilliancy over the face of nature! Then his voice, though mild, pierced to the center, and his words, "I am thy fellow servant," dispelled every fear. We listened—we gazed—we admired! 'Twas the voice of the angel from glory—'twas a message from the Most High! and as we heard we rejoiced, while his love enkindled upon our souls, and we were rapt in the vision of the Almighty! Where was room for doubt? No where: uncertainty had fled, doubt had sunk, no more to rise, while fiction and deception had fled forever!

But, dear brother think, further think for a moment, what joy filled our hearts and with what surprise we must have bowed, (for who would not have bowed the knee for such a blessing?) when

---

*John the Baptist. See D&C 13.

†The Aaronic Priesthood was restored on 15 May 1829.

we received under his hand the holy priesthood, as he said, "upon you my fellow servants, in the name of Messiah I confer this priesthood and this authority, which shall remain upon earth, that the sons of Levi may yet offer an offering unto the Lord in righteousness!"*

I shall not attempt to paint to you the feelings of this heart, nor the majestic beauty and glory which surrounded us on this occasion; but you will believe me when I say, that earth, nor men, with the eloquence of time, cannot begin to clothe language in as interesting and sublime a manner as this holy personage. No; nor has this earth power to give the joy, to bestow the peace, or comprehend the wisdom which was contained in each sentence as they were delivered by the power of the Holy Spirit! Man may deceive his fellow man; deception may follow deception, and the children of the wicked one may have power to seduce the foolish and untaught, till nought but fiction feeds the many, and the fruit of falsehood carries in its current the giddy to the grave; but one touch with the finger of his love, yes, one ray of glory from the upper world, or one word from the mouth of the Savior, from the bosom of eternity, strikes it all into insignificance, and blots it forever from the mind! The assurance that we were in the presence of an angel; the certainty that we heard the voice of Jesus, and the truth unsullied as it flowed from a pure personage, dictated by the will of God, is to me, past description, and I shall ever look upon this expression of the Savior's goodness with wonder and thanksgiving while I am permitted to tarry, and in those mansions where perfection dwells and sin never comes, I hope to adore in that DAY which shall never cease!

. . . I must close for the present: my candle is quite extinguished, and all nature seems locked in silence, shrouded in

---

*A paraphrase of D&C 13.

129

darkness, and enjoying that repose so necessary to this life. But the period is rolling on when night will close, and those who are found worthy will inherit that city where neither the light of the sun nor moon will be necessary! "For the glory of God will lighten it, and the Lamb will be the light thereof."*

O. Cowdery.

To W. W. Phelps, Esq.

P.S. I shall write you again on the subject of the Conference. O.C.

I will hereafter give you a full history of the rise of this church, up to the time stated in my introduction; which will necessarily embrace the life and character of this brother. I shall therefore leave the history of baptism, &c. till its proper place.

W. W. Phelps's history as a Latter-day Saint is nothing short of amazing. He served as Joseph Smith's scribe during the translation of the Book of Abraham and helped compile the Doctrine and Covenants. He was excommunicated and restored to fellowship twice—once in 1838 to 1840 and once in 1847. He assisted the Prophet Joseph Smith with many different activities during the Nauvoo years. He helped Emma Smith compile the first hymnbook and wrote the text to such hymns as "The Spirit of God," "Now Let Us Rejoice," "Redeemer of Israel," and "Praise to the Man." Before his death in 1872, he served in the Legislative Assembly of the Territory of Utah and was admitted to the Utah Bar.

---

*Revelation 21:23: "And the city had no need of the sun, neither of the moon, to shine in it: for the glory of God did lighten it, and the Lamb is the light thereof."

"There Is No Sacrifice We Will Count Too Great"

BRIGHAM YOUNG TO LUCY MACK SMITH
4 APRIL 1847

In February of 1846, the Saints, many of whom had left homes and belongings in Ohio and Missouri, departed Nauvoo and headed across the frozen Mississippi on their long exodus west. By June they had crossed Iowa and reached Council Bluffs. By September many were also encamped at Winter Quarters, across the Missouri River from Council Bluffs (near present-day Omaha, Nebraska). But the hard trek across Iowa left many pioneers in a malnourished state, and they were unprepared for the bitter winter. "It's a growling, grumbling, devilish, sickly time with us now," wrote Eliza R. Snow.[1] Several hundred Saints died in the winter of 1846–47. Brigham Young, who lost two children of his own* in 1846, declared, "We are willing to take our full share of trouble, trials, losses and crosses, hardships and fatigues, warning and watching, for the kingdom of heaven's sake; and we feel to say: Come, calm or strife, turmoil or peace, life or death, in the name of Israel's God we mean to conquer or die trying."[2]

In January of 1847, Brigham Young received a revelation concerning the organization of the Camp of Israel (see D&C 136), and by April the vanguard company of Saints prepared to head west. With Heber C. Kimball and six of his teams scheduled to leave Winter Quarters on 5 April, and others on subsequent days, Brigham was no doubt laboring to the point of exhaustion the first week of April. There were wagons to be fixed, horses to be shod, sheep and cattle to be rounded up, grain and corn to be packed, and a thousand other details—all in unseasonably cold weather. The Saints were in the habit

---

*Two sons, Joseph and Hyrum, born to Brigham and Louisa Beaman in 1846, apparently died the same year. (Arrington, *Brigham Young*, 420.)

of rising early. Still, at midnight on 4 April, forty-five-year-old Brigham Young dictated the following letter to his clerk, Willard Richards. The letter was to Lucy Mack Smith, the Prophet's mother. She was then seventy-one.

Camp of Israel, Winter Quarters
April 4, 1847—Midnight
Mrs. Lucy Smith
Beloved mother in Israel

Our thoughts, our feelings, our desires, and our prayers to our Heavenly Father in the name of Jesus are often drawn out in your behalf, and we can truly say, increasingly, for we can never forget our beloved brother Joseph, either in this world or in the world to come, for the Lord raised him up to do a great work in these last days. We in common with other Saints have been made partakers of the blessings that flow unto the faithful through obedience to the revelations and councils which have come through him for the salvation of Israel. He with his brother Hyrum have sealed their testimony with their blood, and while we strive to emulate their virtues, we are constantly reminded of their aged mother, whom we feel free to call our mother, knowing the many privations, hardships, toils, fatigues, and weariness which she has been called to endure in connection with her beloved Joseph and other children in establishing the Kingdom of God on Earth.

For a long time we have not known where you were, or what your situation; neither do we now know, but . . . we are led to suspect you are in or about Nauvoo, so that possibly this communication may reach you, and as we are speedily to depart from this place, with other Pioneers, and go Westward over the mountains,*

---

*The vanguard company generally followed the recently published maps of John C. Fremont but still encountered a good deal of unknown territory.

as we shall be led by the Spirit of the Lord, to find a location for a Stake of Zion, we felt that we could not take our leave without addressing a line to Mother Smith to let her know that her children in the gospel have not forgotten her.

Your memory and that of your dear husband, our Father in Israel, is sweet unto us, and ever will be, and that of all your household, whom the Lord has given unto you, for he has given you a family to increase without number, which shall continue, worlds without end, and we rejoice that we are of that number.

The household of faith to which we refer is now almost without number. They are scattered abroad upon the four Quarters of the Earth and upon the Islands of the Sea, and are calling upon us night and day, saying, "Where shall we gather to?" And thy Son, even thy very Son Joseph, while in the bloom of youth and in the full vigor of manhood commanded us, thy children, the unworthy Servants of the Most High, to instruct, to teach, to lead, to guide, to counsel, and to direct those who had received and should receive those things his master the Lord Jesus Christ had given unto him, in all righteousness and faithfulness, and this we have endeavored to do according to the best of our ability, and this we are determined to continue to do, and for this end we leave wife and children and everything dear as life. We are now just ready to depart, to find the place which our Father shall point out to us for a Stake of Zion, where the children of the Kingdom may resort to and build their own houses and inhabit them, plant their own gardens and vineyards and enjoy the fruits thereof, and build a house unto the Most High, where those ordinances can be administered without molestation or distraction that shall bring back again the children of Adam and Eve, Abraham and Sarah, Joseph and Lucy into the presence of the Most High God, even the places that they were destined for from before the foundation of the world. Mother Smith, we know not your particular situation only so far as God makes it manifest unto us but be assured of this that our faith and prayers have been and are and will be for your welfare; we will rejoice in your posterity, and as we have hitherto done so will we continue to bless you by all the earthly means in our power. Your children, the children of the Kingdom, are [illegible] in this world's goods, like ourselves. Our Prophet and Patriarch have been martyred, and the children have been driven and scattered, and we have spent our substance to keep them from starvation and destruction, and we are now striving to open the way for the gathering together of the Flock even according to the good will of the Great Shepherd.

There are now thousands and thousands upon thousands who are looking to us continually to open up a way for a shelter from the storm which is about to burst on a world of intelligent beings, who have almost forgotten their God and their Savior, and our time is occupied and our hands are full. But like our Divine Master we have a fulness and yet in his name and by his authority and by his power and by his wisdom we are ready and we are willing to receive all who wish to come. And if our dear Mother Smith should at any time wish to come where the Saints are located and she will make it manifest unto us, there is no sacrifice we will count too great to bring her forward and we ever have been, now are and shall continue to be ready to divide with her the last loaf; and if she chooses not to be with us and we could know where she is we would gladly administer to her wants to the fullest extent that our Heavenly Father would give unto us.

The Lord is blessing his people and will continue to bless them according to their faithfulness and diligence in his [will?] and we feel to rejoice continually in view of the rich blessings. May [Mother Smith's] last days be her best days—may her heart

be satisfied—may she be upheld . . . have all her wants supplied
. . . and may the choicest blessings of heaven abide with you forever, is the prayer of your beloved children in the name of Jesus
Christ, Amen.

> For the Council of the Twelve Apostles
> Brigham Young, President
> Willard Richards, clerk

Lucy Mack Smith had lost her husband, Joseph Sr., in 1840 and her son
Don Carlos in 1841. Then, in the summer of 1844, she lost three more sons in
rapid succession—Joseph and Hyrum on 27 June, and Samuel on 30 July.
When the Saints left Nauvoo in 1846, Lucy, despite serious arthritis, said she
would go west if her children went. However, her sole surviving son (of seven
born to her), William, had been excommunicated in 1845, and none of her
daughters—Sophronia, Katharine, and Lucy—chose to go. So Lucy stayed
behind.

"We left our home just as it was," said Lucy's granddaughter Martha Ann
Smith, daughter of Hyrum and Mary Fielding Smith, who left with the Saints.
"Our furniture, and the fruit trees hanging full of rosy cheeked peaches. We
bid goodbye to the loved home that reminded us of our beloved father everywhere we turned.

"I was five years old when we started from Nauvoo. We crossed over the
Mississippi in the skiff in the dusk of the evening. We bid goodbye to our dear
old feeble grandmother [Lucy Mack Smith]. I can never forget the bitter tears
she shed when she bid us goodbye for the last time in this life. She knew it
would be the last time she would see her son's family. We did not realize this
so much at that time as we have since."[3]

Lucy soon went to live with her daughter and son-in-law Lucy and Arthur
Millikin, about seventy miles north of Nauvoo. She was probably there when
Brigham Young wrote the above letter. In 1851, Lucy went to live with Emma,
whose second husband, Lewis Bidamon, made Lucy a wheelchair when she

could no longer walk. One visitor wrote, "She made a great impression on me for she is no ordinary woman. . . . She is a character that Walter Scott would have loved to portray and he would have done justice to her. . . . She blessed us with a mother's blessing, her own words, and my heart melted."[4]

On Wednesday, 14 May 1856, Lucy Mack Smith died at the age of eighty-one.

"One Stumble Would Have Plunged Us a Thousand Feet Down"

LORENZO SNOW TO FRANKLIN D. RICHARDS
18 FEBRUARY 1852

The remarkable missionary Lorenzo Snow was born in Mantua, Ohio, in 1814 and reared in a well-to-do home. Joseph Smith visited the home in 1831, and Lorenzo's mother and older sister Leonora were baptized. Four years later, Eliza, another older sister of Lorenzo, was baptized. At her encouragement, Lorenzo went to Kirtland, where he was baptized by Apostle John F. Boynton.*

Over the next decade and a half, Lorenzo served missions to Ohio, Kentucky, Illinois, and Missouri. In 1840, while serving a three-year mission to Britain, he presented a copy of the Book of Mormon to Queen Victoria. He would later serve a mission to Hawaii with Joseph F. Smith and Ezra T. Benson and almost drown in a boating accident in 1864.

Lorenzo Snow was ordained an apostle in February of 1849, and in the fall of that year he was called to open a mission in Italy. (At the same time, fellow Apostles John Taylor and Erastus Snow received similar calls to take the gospel to France and Scandinavia.) Lorenzo arrived in Italy in June of 1850 and supervised the translation of the Book of Mormon into Italian. He also supervised the work in Switzerland, and after making a treacherous trip from Geneva, through the tip of France and across the Graian Alps into Turin (in northwest Italy), he wrote the following letter to Apostle Franklin D. Richards, president of the European Mission. Elder Snow was thirty-seven,

---

*One of the original members of the Quorum of the Twelve, John F. Boynton was excommunicated in 1837 and died 20 October 1890 at age seventy-nine.

and Elder Richards, father of George F. Richards and grandfather of both LeGrand and Franklin D. Richards, was thirty.

ITALY, FEBRUARY 18, 1852.

Dear President Richards:

Bidding farewell to Brother and Sister Stenhouse* and the Swiss Saints, I left Geneva on the 9th inst. by *malle poste*, and commenced winding my way over a rough, hilly and mountainous country that formed a strange contrast with the beautiful, undulating *pays* of southern France. As we approached the towering Alps, there came a heavy snow storm, which made our journey very gloomy, dreary and altogether disagreeable. About six o'clock in the evening of the following day, we commenced the ascent of Mount Cenis, and reached its cloudy summit, six thousand seven hundred feet in height, at one o'clock the next morning.

Though but one passenger Beside myself saw proper to venture over the mountain, it was found that ten horses were barely sufficient to carry us forward through the drifting snow, which had fallen to nearly the depth of four feet since the last post had passed, a circumstance that rendered it very dangerous making our way up the narrow road and short turnings. One stumble or the least unlucky toss of our vehicle would, at very many points of our path, have plunged us a thousand feet down rocky precipices.

It may be noticed to the credit of the government that "houses of recovery" are now erected in the dangerous portion of this route, for the preservation and benefit of travelers that may lose their way or be caught in a storm, and their progress hindered

---

*Lorenzo Snow had ordained Thomas B. H. Stenhouse in November of 1850 as the first president of the Swiss Mission.

by the drifting snows. In going the distance of a half mile, six or eight of these benevolent buildings may be seen. We descended the mountain with much more ease to our horses, and more comfort to ourselves; and I felt thankful that my passage over these rocky steeps was completed, and hoped it might never be my lot to cross them a third time at night in the winter season; but regarding these matters, we need seek to exercise no anxiety, inasmuch as over them we hold no control.

On reaching Turin, I had the happiness of meeting Elders [Jabez] Woodard and Joseph Toronto,* and the day following of paying a visit to the Saints in Angrogna.†

I could see and feel that the brethren here had all been baptized into the same Spirit. At a very interesting "re-union," one sister said, "Mr. Snow, it is the first time I see you with my bodily eyes, but the Lord gave me a manifestation a few weeks ago, in which I saw you as plain as I see you now." Another bore testimony of an open vision which she had a short time before. A brother also testified of several cases of healing which had occurred in his own family.

I feel to commend the course pursued by Elder Woodard, whose operations have been directed by wisdom and prudence. Here a branch of the Church has been raised up under circumstances which would have paralyzed the efforts of any one not in possession of the most unshaken confidence in the power of the Lord. We published books at the risk of coming in collision with the government. The Catholic priests called on the ministers of state to prevent their sale; but in spite of every obstacle, we have disposed of nearly all we printed. We are not permitted to preach

---

*Elder Joseph Toronto was one of the first missionaries to Italy, with Elders Snow and Stenhouse.

†Angrogne, Italy, where a branch of the Church had been organized.

in public, and at every step find ourselves far off from the religious liberty enjoyed in England. But Italy is not silent under the shackles of spiritual despotism. Many noble sentiments, and liberal ideas, have been spread through the country by the speeches of honest-hearted men in Parliament, who have called loudly for religious freedom, and we trust they will not always call in vain.

The mission, up to this time, has been necessarily carried on in a narrow sphere, but more favorable openings now seem to present themselves, and the Book of Mormon will lend its powerful aid in building up the Church. After many anxieties with regard to that work, it was no small pleasure to find it welcomed by the Saints in Italy as a heavenly treasure, and the translation so highly approved. Nor can I express the delight which I experienced in gazing upon Mount Brigham, on whose rocky brow we had organized *La Chiesa di Gesu Christo dei Santi degli Ultimi Gioni, in Italia*.

The Waldenses* were the first to receive the Gospel, but by the press and the exertions of the Elders, it will be rolled forth beyond their mountain regions. At this season they are surrounded with snow from three to six feet deep, and in many instances all communication is cut off between the villages. Our labors in such countries will be eminently blessed when we can have persons in the Priesthood who are not under the same disadvantages and liabilities as foreign Elders, and such are rising up here.

Elder John D. Malan, president of the branch, is a man of God, and having labored faithfully under the counsel of Elder Woodard, I think it wisdom that he should take charge of the

---

*The Waldenses were Protestants of French origin. Because of religious persecution they had sought refuge in the Alps.

work here, while Elder Woodard opens the mission in the seaport of Nice. Italian states are well known as being the most hostile upon earth to the introduction of religious truth, but as their subjects are in constant communication with many countries that are washed by the Mediterranean, they will have facilities for hearing the Gospel as we come into connection with their maritime relations; and being acquainted with all the languages around that central sea, the thousands of Italians who perform business upon its waters will furnish some faithful men to speed on the Kingdom of God, through the south and east of Europe. At Nice we shall be able to keep up connection with the Waldenses on one hand and the Maltese on the other. Malta* will be an important field of labor, not only for Italy, but also for Greece, where, according to ancient tradition, a branch of the House of Israel long remained.

The Turkish and Russian empires may also be reached through the same medium; and I hope to see the day when the countries I have named will all be cut up into conferences of Latter-day Saints. Brother Obray will join his labors with those of Brother Woodard, for both Nice and Malta, and for the extension of the mission into other parts of Italy.

As soon as circumstances permit, I shall be moving forward to other realms, and from whence my next communication will proceed, I cannot say; perhaps from Malta, or the crumbling monuments of ruined Egypt, or the burning climes of India.

---

*Malta is a group of islands in the Mediterranean Sea south of Sicily. Elder Snow visited Malta proper, the same island where the apostle Paul was shipwrecked. (See Acts 27–28; the island was then called Melita.)

Praying that the Lord may always be with you, granting you His richest favors,

I remain, as ever, yours affectionately,
LORENZO SNOW.

Although Lorenzo Snow hoped to see India and preach the gospel there, he was called home by the First Presidency—Brigham Young, Heber C. Kimball, and Willard Richards. He reached Salt Lake City on 30 August 1852, almost three years after his departure, and made the following entry in his journal:

"Arriving at my home in Salt Lake City, the long anticipated oasis of this portion of my life-journey the beacon light which succeeded my arduous missionary labors, and shone with a brighter beam than all other earthly luminaries, the happiness of once again meeting my loved and loving family would have been full, but alas! there was a sad vacancy. A lovely one was not; one who ever met me with a smiling face and a loving heart, was not there to respond to love's sacred call; Charlotte,* my dear wife, had been stricken down by death, and her beautiful form lay mouldering in the silent tomb. Yet there Was Consolation in the thought that her pure spirit was mingling with holy beings above. A short time after Charlotte's decease, while I was in Italy, a sister in London, a very faithful Saint, the wife of Elder Jabez Woodard, had an open vision, in which she saw a beautiful woman, the most lovely being she ever beheld, clothed in white robes and crowned with glory. This personage told Mrs. Woodard that she was a wife of Lorenzo Snow."[1]

---

*Charlotte Merrill Squires was Lorenzo Snow's first wife. They were married in the Nauvoo Temple on 17 January 1846 and had two daughters. She died on 25 September 1850, at age twenty-four or twenty-five.

"The Inspiration of Heaven Is Directing You"

ELIZA R. SNOW TO AURELIA SPENCER ROGERS
4 AUGUST 1878

Aurelia Spencer was born in Deep River, Connecticut, in 1834. Seven years later the family joined the Church and settled in Nauvoo. During the winter of 1845–46, when Aurelia was eleven years old, the Saints were forced to flee Nauvoo. She later recalled that experience: "My mother had scarcely recovered from a spell of sickness, which followed the death of little Chloe [a baby sister], and was illy prepared to stand the cold weather and rough roads we had to travel over in the fore part of the journey. She therefore gradually sank from the effects of a severe cold and soon died. As we had only traveled a distance of thirty miles, her body was taken back to Nauvoo and buried. . . . This was my first great sorrow. We missed her very much."[1]

Aurelia and the other children eventually traveled to Utah with an early pioneer company while their father, Orson Spencer, served a mission to England. In 1851, Aurelia married Thomas Rogers, and they moved to Farmington, Utah. They had twelve children, five of whom died as infants. When Thomas was called on a mission, Aurelia baked a dozen loaves of bread a day, made the family's clothes by hand, and labored in the fields to support the family.

In 1878, forty-three-year-old Aurelia became concerned with the behavior of young boys. She expressed these concerns in a letter to Eliza R. Snow and asked, "Could there not be an organization for little boys and have them trained to make better men?" Aurelia also concluded that the meeting would not be complete without the girls.[2] The seventy-four-year-old general president of the Relief Society, Eliza R. Snow, sent the following reply.

SALT LAKE CITY, AUG. 4, 1878

My dear sister Rogers: The spirit and contents of your letter pleased me much. I feel assured that the inspiration of heaven is directing you, and that a great and very important movement is being inaugurated for the future of Zion.

Your letter was waiting my return from Provo Valley on Thursday evening—yesterday (Sat.) I read it in our general meeting in the Fourteenth Ward Assembly Rooms.

Soon after my return from Farmington I proposed to Sister Mary J. Thompson to move forward in the Sixteenth Ward and establish a president, requesting her to suggest a whole souled brother who would enter into the spirit of the work; and last evening with her, I called on Brother Perkins, whose feelings were fully enlisted as soon as we informed him of the object in question. He is in daily employment during the week, and although a constant attendant at Sabbath service is willing to devote the afternoon to the benefit of the children, and for the time being deprive himself of the enjoyment of the Sacrament. The importance of the movement, and its great necessity is fully acknowledged by all with whom I have conversed on the subject.

President John Taylor* fully approbates it, and President Joseph F. Smith† thinks we might better afford what expenses might be incurred in furnishing uniform, musical instruments etc, for the cultivation of the children in Zion, than what we are expending in converting people abroad where elders spend years in converting a very few.

---

*John Taylor, the senior apostle in the Church, had been president of the Quorum of the Twelve since the death of Brigham Young a year earlier. He was ordained President of the Church in 1880.

†Joseph F. Smith had served as a counselor to the First Presidency from 1867 until Brigham Young's death in 1877. He was called as second counselor in the First Presidency when John Taylor was ordained President of the Church.

We think that at present, it will be wisdom to not admit any under six years of ag[e], except in some special instances. You are right—we must have the girls as well as the boys—they must be trained together.

I think your mind will be directed to a brother who will unite with you in establishing this movement. Brother Perkins thinks that plenty of assistance will be forthcoming as the work progresses. The angels and all holy beings, especially the leaders of Israel on the other side [of] the veil will be deeply interested.

I wish to see and converse with you, but cannot make it convenient at present. Tomorrow is election—on the 6th, if the Lord wills I shall go to Mendon—attend the sisters' Quarterly Conference in Ogden on the 15th and 16th—go to West Porterville on the 17th and return hom[e] sometime about the 20th. If I can so arrange will see you on my return.

That God will continue to inspire you in the establishment and development of this great movement, is the earnest prayer of

Your sister and fellow laborer,

E. R. Snow

One week after this letter was written, on 11 August 1878, Aurelia Spencer Rogers became the first ward Primary president in the Church. On 25 August a chapel full of children met in the Farmington Ward for the first Primary meeting. The next month, Eliza R. Snow nominated Louie B. Felt to be president of the Salt Lake City 11th Ward Primary, and she became the second ward Primary president.

Two years later Sister Felt was called as the first general president of the Primary. Although she was childless herself, Sister Felt had a remarkable influence on the children of the Church, serving as president for forty-five years.

In 1911, Sister Felt and her second counselor, May Anderson (who later served as president herself), encountered a young crippled boy on the streets of Salt Lake City. This experience was the catalyst for their recommendation that a children's convalescent hospital be established. That same year, the Primary sponsored a children's ward in LDS Hospital. Sister Felt then oversaw fund-raising and construction of a new hospital, which opened its doors in 1922. Thirty years later a much larger Primary Children's Hospital was constructed.

Sister Felt also introduced innovative teaching techniques, activities such as singing, dance, and drama, and the *Children's Friend* magazine. Today more than a million and a half children are members of Primary, which is responsible for all formal religious instruction of LDS children.

"I Love the People of God with All the Power of My Being"

HEBER J. GRANT TO AMY BROWN LYMAN
27 NOVEMBER 1918

In 1917, the Church sent Amy Brown Lyman, general secretary of the Relief Society and an experienced social worker, to the National Conference of Charities and Correction. Implementing many of the methods she studied at the conference, Amy founded the Relief Society Social Service Department in 1919. The department offered a variety of services to women, including an employment bureau, training in social work, foster care, and adoption services. In these efforts, Sister Lyman was particularly encouraged by Apostle Heber J. Grant, a good friend of Amy's husband, distinguished engineer Richard R. Lyman.

Heber J. Grant and Richard's father, Francis M. Lyman, had served together in the Quorum of the Twelve for thirty-four years, with Elder Grant succeeding Elder Lyman as president of the Quorum when the latter died in 1916. Their friendship went back to their preapostle days in the early 1880s, when eleven-year-old Richard had driven teams for both of them. Richard and twenty-five-year-old Heber ate candy and raisins and talked as they rode together, forming a lifelong bond. As an adult, Richard became director of Heber J. Grant and Company.[1]

On 6 April 1918, forty-seven-year-old Richard R. Lyman was called to the Quorum of the Twelve. Seven months later, on 19 November, President Joseph F. Smith died at age eighty. Heber J. Grant was ordained President of the Church on 23 November 1918, at age sixty-two. Four days later, he wrote the following letter to Amy Brown Lyman, forty-six.

November 27th, 1918

Mrs. Amy Brown Lyman,

Denver, Colo.

My dear Amy:

Your letter of the 24th received yesterday afternoon. I have had many splendid letters of congratulations since my call to the Presidency of the Church came, but not one which I prized more highly than yours. I thank you for it from the bottom of my heart. I know there is not one word of love, confidence or congratulations but what you feel just what you say. This is what makes your letter so dear to my heart. It is just such support as the faith and prayers of faithful saints like yourself which makes the duties of President of the Church a joy beyond expression.

I start this afternoon at 4:45 with Gusta* for Santa Monica. Have been suffering with insomnia for more than a week, and we are making the trip for fear of a breakdown on my part before I get really started in my new labors.

If you are right that no one is more "greatly beloved by the people" than your humble servant, I pray that I may so live as to retain this love of the people. I believe that there is nothing truer than the saying, "We love to be loved." I do love the people of God with all the power of my being, and your words are very precious to me when you tell of their love for me. Next time you write don't you fail to tell all the good things you may wish for fear of infringing on my time—"I like it."

None of the wives of the Apostles, I am sure, are more dear to Gusta's heart than you and somehow I generally love everyone Gusta loves, including myself.

I thank you for your prayer that I may have a long life, and I

---

*Hulda Augusta Winters Grant, Heber J. Grant's second wife. They were married on 26 May 1884.

know that "the prayers of the righteous availeth much." Your beloved husband, with the aid of your son [Wendell], is doing much to lighten my labors by dictating replies to nearly every one of my personal letters to the machine for Wendell to transcribe.

Pardon me for "infringing" on your time. I know you are a busy woman. I have written this letter with a pencil, sitting up in bed, and shall have Wendell copy it while Richard and I are in our Council meeting. I have other letters to write, and you, dear Amy, have really had very much more than the average time which I have given to my dear friends in replying to the many splendid letters which have come to hand since my call to the Presidency. Susie and Delia* are with us. Susie is quite sick and Delia has to take care of her.

I love you and I say from the bottom of my heart, "<u>God bless you and your loved ones now and forever.</u>"

Yours affectionately,
Heber J. Grant

Amy Brown Lyman's wonderful life of service was laced with tragedy. She and Richard both suffered from health problems, and Amy lost a kidney. Her son Wendell, mentioned in the letter, married Rachel Ballif in 1924, but Rachel died two years later, leaving an eight-month-old daughter. Seven years later, in 1933, Wendell, thirty-five, also died, and Richard and Amy became parents to their granddaughter.

But perhaps the heaviest cross came in 1943, three years after Heber J. Grant called Amy to be general president of the Relief Society. In November of that year, Richard R. Lyman, an apostle for more than twenty-five years and

---

*A reference to Gusta's younger sister Susan Marian Winters Bennion, and older sister Delia Ina Winters Booth.

fifth in seniority in the Quorum,* was excommunicated for violation of the law of chastity.†

Amy continued as Relief Society general president, a task that grew increasingly difficult. The Lymans' dear friend Heber J. Grant had been partially incapacitated by a stroke in 1940 and was largely inactive when Amy submitted her resignation in the fall of 1944. She was honorably released six months later.

At the April 1942 general conference, President Grant spoke in public for the last time. His biographer remarks that during his last years "he called three new members of the Twelve who ultimately became Presidents of the Church: Harold B. Lee, Spencer W. Kimball, and Ezra Taft Benson. He also called Mark E. Petersen to the Twelve during this period to fill the vacancy caused by the excommunication of Richard R. Lyman. The fall of Elder Lyman was one of the great sorrows of his life.

"Near the end of 1944 the prophet's health began to weaken. He discontinued making his daily diary entries. His condition continued to wane until May 14, 1945, when he quietly passed away. Because of his advanced age and his life of achievement and service, the funeral was almost like a valedictory. As the funeral procession proceeded east on South Temple, the bells of the Catholic cathedral at Third East tolled their acknowledgement while the priests stood on the sidewalk to bid farewell to their friend. The prophet was laid to rest in the cemetery high on the east bench, overlooking the valley he loved."[2]

---

*In November of 1943, the members of the Twelve were George Albert Smith, George F. Richards, Joseph Fielding Smith, Stephen L Richards, Richard R. Lyman, John A. Widtsoe, Joseph F. Merrill, Charles A. Callis, Albert E. Bowen, Harold B. Lee, Spencer W. Kimball, and Ezra Taft Benson. Elders Kimball and Benson had been ordained one month earlier.

†Richard R. Lyman was rebaptized in 1954 by Elder Marion D. Hanks.

"Many . . . Shall Rise Up and Call You Blessed"

JAMES E. TALMAGE TO CHARLES A. CALLIS
5 SEPTEMBER 1931

~

Born of English parents in Ireland, Charles A. Callis lived a life of remarkable missionary service. He served a mission to Great Britain in the 1890s. A decade later he took his wife, Grace, and his young family on a mission to the Southern states, serving from 1906 to 1908. Then, just one month after his release, he was called as president of the Southern States Mission and returned with his family to Tennessee, where he supervised a mission that stretched from southern Ohio to Virginia to Florida. "Meanwhile his years as president increased and lengthened out their time. Past the first three years, throughout the war years, into the days of the Roaring Twenties when much of America remained a giddy fanfare of business prosperity, and well into the agonizing, terrible daze of the depression—and still Charles A. Callis and his devoted wife remained in the South."[1]

President Callis, sixty-six, was in his twenty-fourth year as mission president when he received the following letter from James E. Talmage, sixty-eight, who, like President Callis, had been born in the British Isles and immigrated to the United States as a young teenager. Elder Talmage had been a member of the Quorum of the Twelve since 1911 and had written such influential works as *The Articles of Faith, The House of the Lord,* and *Jesus the Christ.*

~

September 5, 1931
President Charles A. Callis
Southern States Mission
485 North Avenue, N. E.
Atlanta, Georgia
Personal

Dear President Callis:

The enclosures are in line with those sent to all Mission Presidents in North America.

Word of your having been called to undergo a surgical operation for appendicitis brought great concern to all your brethren here, but this feeling was mingled with one of faith and confidence that all shall be well with you.

At our Council meeting on Thursday last you were remembered especially and most fervently before the Lord at the altar, and I am sure you are never forgotten in either the secret or family prayers offered by your brethren.

Your work is that of a great leader in Israel, and the extent of it you do not, because you can not, comprehend; but it will be unfolded to you in its full measure as you hear your name acclaimed in the presence of the Lord by the many who shall rise up and call you blessed. But this great consummation is yet far off, as we reckon years, for I am sure your work on earth lies yet largely before you, in effectiveness if not in time duration.

It is your blessing, my Brother, that the evil one shall never have power to shorten your days, for you are to live until you have finished every whit of the work the Lord would have you do.

Kindly extend my very best regards to Sister Callis and your household, both family and official, and be assured of the ever-sustaining faith and supplications of your fellow servants.

Cordially your brother,
James E. Talmage

Enc 3

⎯

Elder Talmage's prophecy of future service saw profound fulfillment. Two years after writing this letter, Elder Talmage died at age seventy. The man called to fill the vacancy in the Quorum of the Twelve was none other than

Charles A. Callis, who was sustained at the general conference in October 1933. He was called with no advance warning, a common practice with President Heber J. Grant. "The appointment came unexpectedly and we were filled with almost overcoming surprise," Elder Callis wrote to family members.[2]

At sixty-eight, Elder Callis was the oldest man called to the Twelve in more than a quarter century. Apostle George Albert Smith, later to become President of the Church, wrote to Grace Callis that it had been one of his cherished desires to see Elder Callis become a General Authority.[3] Elder Callis served during the historic years of the Depression and World War II, visiting stakes and missions throughout the Church and delivering a series of lectures over national radio.

The Southern states, where he had labored for twenty-eight years, remained dear to him. He had long yearned for a stake to be created in the area, and at age eighty-one, he had the honor of traveling to his beloved South to organize the first stake, in Jacksonville, Florida, where he and his wife, Grace, had first labored in a branch of twenty people when they were originally called to serve in the South more than thirty years earlier. Grace had died in October of 1946, and on Sunday, 20 January 1947, the evening after he had organized the stake, Elder Callis wrote to his daughter, "I am being treated well but it is very lonely without your mother. . . . The Lord gave me strength to go through with the organization. With his aid I am battling through. I feel that your mother is not far from us."[4] Less than twelve hours later, Charles A. Callis, having finished "every whit" of his work for the Lord, quietly passed away.*

---

*Elder Harold B. Lee assisted Elder Callis in organizing the stake in Florida. Elder Callis's "emotions were close to the surface, and it became apparent to those who were with him that he was preparing for the end of his life. He ordered a room in the church fitted up as a bedroom, and he insisted upon spending two nights alone in that room. He told the brethren that everywhere he went he saw Sister Callis. Elder Lee wrote:

'I had the impression, and so expressed myself to Sister Jenkins, that Brother Callis wanted to die and had wished it could take place in that room, by himself. He had us drive him to the old chapel and to the home where his twin sons were born and died. He seemed to be reliving those experiences for the last time.'" (Goates, 205.)

The day after Charles A. Callis and Elder Lee organized the stake in Jacksonville, Elder Callis was riding in a car with A. O. Jenkins, of the Florida Stake high council, to organize a ward in Georgia. When Elder Callis suddenly stopped speaking and slumped in his seat, Brother Jenkins immediately drove to a hospital less than a block away. Doctors there found that Elder Callis was already gone. Funeral services were held in both Jacksonville and Salt Lake City.

A Plea to Send Missionaries

During the 1950s, pamphlets and other Church literature and copies of the Book of Mormon found their way into the west African countries of Nigeria and Ghana. Independently of each other, several groups of black Africans began to establish congregations, identifying themselves as "The Church of Jesus Christ of Latter-day Saints" and registering with their governments. They held meetings and taught the gospel to the best of their knowledge.

In Ghana in 1964, Joseph W. B. Johnson obtained copies of Joseph Smith's testimony and of the Book of Mormon. "I read the testimony of the Prophet Joseph Smith, and I believed that testimony," Joseph Johnson later recalled. "I read the Book of Mormon and found it to be true—the true word of God." Then one morning, "while about to prepare for my daily work, I heard my name mentioned thrice: 'Johnson, Johnson, Johnson. If you will take up my work as I will command you, I will bless you and bless your land.' Trembling and in tears, I replied, 'Lord, with thy help I will do whatsoever you will command me.' From that day onward, I was constrained by that Spirit to go from street to street and door to door. . . . I did exactly as the Lord commanded me. I couldn't help it, I had to share the message."[1]

Joseph Johnson soon gave his full time to preaching the gospel. From 1964 to 1978 he organized at least ten congregations bearing the Church's name and taught the gospel to hundreds of unbaptized disciples.

Believers in Nigeria had organized into similar congregations, with approximately 15,000 people hoping for baptism. Although Brother and Sister LaMar Williams and other couples were called to serve missions in Nigeria, they encountered serious difficulty trying to obtain visas. Then in 1965, a civil war in Nigeria made such missions impossible.

In 1960, after his release as president of the South Africa Mission, Glen C. Fisher visited "Mormons" in Nigeria and offered this account: "I introduced myself as a Mormon missionary and they immediately reached out and took both my hands. Never have I received a more sincere and enthusiastic welcome. They led me to a chair and for three hours we sat and discussed the teachings of the Church.

"A visit to their churches convinced me that members of the congregation were living in extreme poverty. . . . For a number of years past they had been preparing their congregation for baptism into The Church of Jesus Christ of Latter-day Saints. Their president told me that they had two congregations with a total membership of over a thousand people, and with some pride he declared that not a single one either smoked or used alcoholic beverages. The members also paid tithing and they had been able to accumulate sufficient funds to erect two small chapels."[2]

The following letter is typical of many letters sent from Ghana and Nigeria to Church headquarters during the 1960s and '70s.

—

Sunday Frank Idoh
P O Box 26
Abak, South Eastern State
Nigeria, West Africa
13th March, 1972
The Church of Jesus Christ
Of Latter-day Saints
Missionary Department
47 East South Temple Street
Salt Lake City, Utah 84111
Dear brothers in Christ,
We have the please to inform you of our satisfaction on the restored gosple of Christ as testify by the secred book of mormon

which was reveal through vision to his holiness the Prophet Joseph Smith, and jointly say as followers:—

(1) That we want to have or be come part and parcel of the Church of Jesus Christ of latter-day Saints.

(2) That we believe in Joseph Smiths vision to be true, and believe all that God has revealed.

(3) That we want a branch of the Church Jesus Christ of latter-day Saints to be opened here in our Country (Nigeria).

(4) That a teacher or the Complete doctrine of the Church of Jesus Christ of latter-day Saints be sent to us.

(5) That we want untimely Communication from our brothers all over.

(6) That a visit to us/brothers in Nigeria be arranged.

(7) That we be granted membership into the Church of Jesus Christ of latter-day Saints and the use of the Name Church of Jesus Christ of latter-day Saints on our sign board, together with her Emblem.

We shall rejoice greatly in the Lord on approval of our request above. So act soon for no one knows the day nor the hour when the son of man cometh.

So it is better we walk when we have light least the night come when no man shall see.

Lord Jesus come now come soon.

> Yours brotherly in Christ
> (1) S. F. Idoh (leader)
> (2) E. Jackson (surpporter)
> (3) Ekong Frank (group Committee)
> (4) B. U. Nelson (surpporter)*

---

*In an interview with the author in 2001, former counselor in the International Mission and missionary to Africa Edwin Q. Cannon, who collected these and many other letters, said he did not have specific knowledge of what became of Brothers Idoh, Jackson, Frank, and Nelson.

"We Are Happy for the Many Hours in the Upper Room of the Temple"

OBINNA BROTHERS TO THE FIRST PRESIDENCY
1 DECEMBER 1978

At the same time that Joseph Johnson was preaching in Ghana, Anthony Obinna was being prepared for the gospel in Nigeria. "In November 1965," he later wrote, "I was visited in a dream by a tall person carrying a walking stick in his right hand. He asked whether I had read about Christian and Christiana from *A Pilgrim's Progress* by John Bunyan. I told him that I had forgotten it and he told me to read it again. After a few months the same personage appeared to me again and took me to a most beautiful building and showed me everything in it. That personage appeared to me three times.

"During the Nigerian civil war, when we were confined to the house, I picked up an old copy of the *Reader's Digest* for September 1958. I opened it at page 34 and saw a picture of the same beautiful building I had been shown around in my dream, and immediately I recognized it. The heading was 'The March of the Mormons.' I had never before heard the word *Mormons*. I started to read the story because of the picture of the building I had seen in my dream. I discovered that it was all about The Church of Jesus Christ of Latter-day Saints.

"From the time I finished reading the story, I had no rest of mind any longer. My whole attention was focused on my new discovery. I rushed out immediately to tell my brothers, who were all amazed and astonished to hear the story.

"By that time there was a blockade all over Nigeria, so I could not write any letters to the headquarters of the Church. At the removal of the blockade in 1971 I wrote a letter for instructions. Pamphlets, tracts, and a Book of

Mormon were sent to me, including 'Joseph Smith's Testimony' about the restoration of the gospel. Brother LaMar S. Williams was in the Missionary Department at that time, and his instructions were that they had no authority to organize the Church in Nigeria then. I was totally disappointed, but the Holy Spirit moved me to continue writing. Many a time in dreams I saw some of the missionaries of the Church discussing matters about the Church.

"Persecutions, name calling, and all kinds of abuses were rendered to me. I was persecuted in various ways but I kept deaf ears. I knew I had discovered the truth and men's threats could not move me and my group. So we continued asking God to open the door for us."[3]

In June of 1978, Spencer W. Kimball, N. Eldon Tanner, and Marion G. Romney of the First Presidency announced that a revelation had been received by President Kimball extending the priesthood to all worthy male members. Six months later, Anthony Obinna and his brothers sent the following letter to the First Presidency:

The Church of Jesus Christ of L. D. S. Mission
Umuelem Enyioguru - Aboh Mbaise Branch
Owerri. Imo State - Nigeria
West Africa
1st December, 1978
The Church of Jesus Christ of L. D. S.,
The Office of the First Presidency,
Salt Lake City, Utah 84150
U.S.A.
Dear Brethren,
The entire members of the Church of Jesus Christ of Latter Day Saints in this part of Nigeria have the pleasure to thank you and the Latter Day Saints throughout the world for opening the door for the Gospel to come to our people in its fulness.

We are happy for the many hours in the Upper Room of the

Temple you spent supplicating the Lord to bring us into the fold. We thank our Heavenly Father for hearing your prayers and ours and by revelation has confirmed the long promised day, and has granted the holy priesthood to us, with the power to exercise its divine authority and enjoy every blessing of the temple.

Nineteen members were baptized and confirmed on the 21/11/78 being Tuesday by—Randell N. Mabey, Edwin Q. Cannon, Dr. A. Bruce Knudsen* etc. with their honourable ladies who made the day most enjoyable in our lives.

Three members of the Church were ordained to the priesthood and the 4th was ordained a teacher.

We thank the women members of the Church for making Mrs. Fidelia Obinna the leader of the Relief Society for this area. The delegates from Salt Lake City, I believe will tell you about their observations of us, and places they visited.

We are still happier to have Dr. A. Bruce Knudsen and his wife as our Regional Administrator of the Church. There is no doubt that the Church here will grow and become a mighty centre for the Saints and bring progress enough to the people of Nigeria as it is doing all over the world.

We thank you for extending the priesthood which has been withheld to us and to prepare us to receive every blessing of the gospel.

May God continue to bless you now and always.

> Sincerely yours,
> Anthony U. Obinna
> Francis I. Obinna
> Raymond I. Obinna

---

*Dr. A. Bruce Knudsen, employed by the World Health Organization in a mosquito-abatement research project, was in Nigeria with his family.

cc: Edwin Q. Cannon
Randell N. Mabey
Dr. A. Bruce Knudsen

———

In discussing the revelation on the priesthood, President Kimball said: "We had the glorious experience of having the Lord indicate clearly that the time had come when all worthy men and women everywhere can be fellowheirs and partakers of the full blessings of the gospel. I want you to know, as a special witness of the Savior, how close I have felt to him and to our Heavenly Father as I have made numerous visits to the upper rooms in the temple, going on some days several times by myself. The Lord made it very clear to me what was to be done. We do not expect the people of the world to understand such things, for they will always be quick to assign their own reasons or to discount the divine process of revelation."[4]

Two months after the revelation was announced, in August of 1978, Edwin Q. Cannon, a counselor in the International Mission, and Merrill Bateman, later a member of the First Quorum of the Seventy and president of BYU, traveled to western Africa on a fact-finding tour. Two months after that, Elder Cannon and his wife, Janath, and Rendell and Rachel Mabey arrived in Nigeria as representatives of the International Mission. (Elders Cannon and Mabey had both previously served as mission presidents in Europe with responsibility for Church members not included in other missions.)

Anthony Obinna was the first person baptized in Nigeria. He was also called as president of the Aboh Branch, with his brothers Francis and Raymond as counselors. The Cannons and Mabeys soon traveled to Ghana, where Joseph Johnson was baptized and became Ghana's first branch president. Within a year, more than 1,700 people had joined the Church in Nigeria and Ghana.

As of the year 2000, there were more than 42,000 members of the Church in Nigeria and more than 17,000 in Ghana. President Gordon B. Hinckley visited both countries in 1998, spoke to thousands of Saints, and announced temples for each country.

Elder Alexander B. Morrison, emeritus member of the First Quorum of the Seventy, writes: "A new day is dawning over Africa because God in His wisdom wills it to be so, and that makes all the difference. In many ways the key to it all—or at least the signal of divine intentions—was the revelation on the priesthood in 1978. That symbol of God's love for all of His children signified that a critical point had been reached in the divine timetable for earth and its inhabitants, and that the time had come to call up the last laborers to serve in the vineyard of the Lord."[5]

"We Were All Touched by the Talk of Brother McConkie"

GORDON B. HINCKLEY TO J. WILLARD MARRIOTT
17 APRIL 1985

—

In January of 1985, the First Presidency of Spencer W. Kimball, Marion G. Romney, and Gordon B. Hinckley invited members of the Church in the United States and Canada to observe a special fast day (27 January), abstain from two meals, and donate the equivalent value, or more, to assist famine-stricken people in Africa. Three months later, in general conference, second counselor President Hinckley thanked members of the Church and said they had "responded in a magnificent way in sharing [their] plenty with those who are destitute."

"The response of those who participated has been wonderful. It has been most gratifying. . . . Your contributions have reached the sum of $6,025,656." President Hinckley further reported that $4.4 million had been given to such agencies as the American Red Cross, Catholic Relief Services, and CARE.

"How grateful we are for the inspiration of the Almighty in establishing so simple, yet so effective a program for relieving want and suffering."[1]

Two weeks later, President Hinckley, seventy-four, sent the following letter to his good friend J. Willard Marriott, eighty-four.

—

April 17, 1985
Mr. J. Willard Marriott
5302 East Lincoln Drive
Scottsdale, AZ 85253
Dear Bill:
Thank you for your letter of 9 April, with enclosed check in

163

the sum of $5,000.00 sent as a contribution to assist the starving people of Africa. An official receipt will be sent to you, but I hasten to send this note of appreciation.

As I reported in the general conference, great good has been done in meeting the urgent needs of many in that distressed part of the world.

I appreciate your generous words concerning the conference. We were all richly blessed. It was good to have President Kimball with us during four sessions and President Romney was able to get there for one session.

We were all touched by the talk of Brother McConkie. He put his whole strength into that effort. He has not been to the office since, and his condition has worsened. The prognosis is not good.

I hope that you and Allie* are getting along well, and enjoying a good measure of health and vitality. Please be assured of our love.

Sincerely,

Gordon

Gordon B. Hinckley

In many ways, this brief letter was a portent of future events. The Church held another special fast day in November of 1985, and Church members again responded generously. President Thomas S. Monson later said, "An example of humanitarian aid can be seen in the Church's response in 1985 to the needs of famine-stricken Ethiopia. As the suffering there became apparent, our members in the United States and Canada were invited to participate

---

*Alice Sheets Marriott. She and J. Willard Marriott were married on 9 June 1927. One of their early business ventures was an A & W ("Allie and Willard") root beer stand. She died on 18 April 2000 at age ninety-two.

in two special fast days. The contributions went to this cause. The proceeds received from these two fast days exceeded $11 million dollars and provided much-needed aid to the people in Ethiopia, Chad, and other sub-Saharan nations. Not one cent was deducted for overhead, for that was also an offering. The funds were not invested to obtain interest. Rather, they were given freely to meet the need."[2]

As the letter indicates, President Spencer W. Kimball and President Marion G. Romney were both in poor health at the April 1985 conference. Neither of them spoke at the conference—and neither would speak at any subsequent conferences. President Kimball died seven months later, on 5 November 1985, at age ninety. With President Kimball's death, President Romney was released from the First Presidency, and he returned to the Quorum of the Twelve as its president. Because of President Romney's ill health, however, Acting President of the Twelve, Howard W. Hunter, handled administrative duties. President Romney died on 20 May 1988, also at age ninety.

As President Hinckley mentioned in his letter, Elder Bruce R. McConkie, who had been battling colon cancer for more than a year, bore a powerful testimony. In the closing remarks of his address, "The Purifying Power of Gethsemane," Elder McConkie declared, "I am one of [Christ's] witnesses, and in a coming day I shall feel the nail marks in his hands and in his feet and shall wet his feet with my tears.

"But I shall not know any better then than I know now that he is God's Almighty Son, that he is our Savior and Redeemer, and that salvation comes in and through his atoning blood and in no other way.

"God grant that all of us may walk in the light as God our Father is in the light so that, according to the promises, the blood of Jesus Christ his Son will cleanse us from all sin."[3]

Two days after President Hinckley wrote the above letter, Elder McConkie died at age sixty-nine.

Just four months after the letter was written, J. Willard Marriott himself passed away, on 13 August 1985, of an apparent heart attack. He was eighty-four. Speaking at the funeral in the Washington, D.C., Stake Center (along with Ezra Taft Benson, Boyd K. Packer, former President Richard Nixon, and the Reverend Billy Graham), President Hinckley said, "His faith was simple and his love of God profound. No one will know of the vast good he did. . . . He gave of his time and strength and means. His hallmark was serving and his standard was integrity."[4]

"You Took the Time to Come to My Family"

VANCE TAYLOR TO HOWARD W. HUNTER
16 JANUARY 1992

Howard W. Hunter had served as a bishop and stake president and had a thriving law practice when he was called to the Quorum of the Twelve in 1959, at age fifty-one. During his thirty-five years as an apostle, Elder Hunter served as president of the Genealogical Society and the Polynesian Cultural Center. He became known for his tact and his ability to deal with people genuinely and kindly. As an emissary of the First Presidency, he spent more than a decade negotiating with Israeli officials for a site for the BYU Jerusalem Center for Near Eastern Studies. Jeffrey R. Holland, then president of BYU, later said that "without President Howard W. Hunter . . . there would have been no BYU Jerusalem Center."[1]

Elder Hunter also served as Church historian and managing director of the Church Historical Department. Leonard Arrington, the only Church historian who was not a General Authority, described a key meeting with Elder Hunter: "He was very relaxed and friendly. He said . . . that he felt the church was mature enough that our history should be honest. Our faith should not overpower our collective memories and documented experiences. He did not believe in suppressing information, hiding documents, or concealing or withholding minutes for 'screening.' . . . I accepted [Elder Hunter's] counsel as a mandate for free and honest scholarly pursuit, with a warning that we must be discreet."[2]

Elder Hunter and his wife, Claire Jeffs Hunter, both suffered a series of serious health problems. He cared for her during a long illness, and she passed away in 1983. Elder Hunter himself then endured such serious ailments as back surgery, cancer, internal bleeding, and a heart attack. By 1992, when he was serving as president of the Quorum of the Twelve, he had lost the use of his legs. He was eighty-four when he received the following letter from fourteen-year-old Church member Vance Taylor.

January 16, 1992

Dear President Hunter:

Hello! I hope that you will read this letter. First of all, let me tell you that I love you. You are truly great; I know that you are a true apostle of God.

I don't think that you will remember me but I met you in July 1991 in the Church office building.* I met you right when you were coming out of the Quorum of the Twelve conference room. As you came out of the room, you had two men with you, one was Elder Boyd K. Packer[†] and I don't know the other gentleman's name, but as you came out of the room with your walker, my family was watching in [awe]. Instead of you just going straight to the elevator and leaving, you took the time to come to my family and shake all of our hands. Me and my sister Kathy are both in wheelchairs and have trouble raising our hands to shake hands with people but you somehow knew and came straight to our hands and said "hello." You then shook my other sister's (Martha) hand and her husband's (fiancé then) hand.

Right when you shook my mother's you looked in her soul as you did with the others but when you did this to my mother you said "all will be fine." I don't know how you knew but, I was in the office building receiving a blessing from Elder Robert Wells[‡] for a major surgery that I was going to have. When you said that

---

*Actually the Church Administration Building.

[†]Elder Packer was then second in seniority in the Twelve to President Hunter.

[‡]Elder Robert E. Wells was then a member of the First Quorum of the Seventy. He was named an emeritus General Authority in 1997.

we truly knew that "all would be fine." Now that my surgery is over, it was a big success. It was a medical miracle just as Elder Wells had promised. I would like for you to know that whenever I doubt something these words "all will be fine" come into my mind and I know everything will be fine.

I love you and support and sustain you. I pray for you always, I know that you probably won't have time to write me back but, if you could, I would appreciate it very much. I would like very much to thank you for asking Elder Packer to show my family the Quorum of the Twelve meeting room and President Benson's office. It was truly a glorious day for me and my family.

Love,

Vance Taylor*

My son Vance is fourteen years old. I thought it would be easier for you to read his letter typed. I love you, Vance's mom.

When President Benson died in June 1994, President Hunter became the fourteenth President of the Church. Preaching the principle that he himself had lived so well, he said, "I would invite all members of the Church to live with ever more attention to the life and example of the Lord Jesus Christ, especially the love and hope and compassion He displayed. I pray that we might treat each other with more kindness, more courtesy, more humility and patience and forgiveness."[3]

President Hunter died on 3 March 1995, at age eighty-seven, two months after an announcement that he had prostate cancer that had spread to the bone. His good friend Elder Jon M. Huntsman bade farewell at the funeral:

"Thank you, dear President, for permitting us to learn from your humility and graciousness. How often you quietly listened while others were telling you

---

*As of the winter of 2001, Vance Taylor was a senior at Brigham Young University. He reported that he sent two letters to President Hunter and received personal replies both times.

something you already knew—and yet you thanked them, complimented them, and made them feel so very important. You were such a kind and thoughtful listener. You possessed a remarkable and quick sense of humor, particularly during times of physical or emotional stress or illness. It would always manifest itself in such delightful ways. To those who helped you to the podium, you would often say, 'Brethren, I hope next time you won't need my help.' To those helping you to your seat afterwards, you would quietly whisper, 'Just drop me anyplace.' . . .

"Dear President, you always followed the Savior's admonition to turn the other cheek (see Matt. 5:39) if others offended you, and you so ably taught us to honorably bear and revere the priesthood of God, that it is, indeed, the most treasured gift on earth, far more valuable than either position or possessions.

"Thank you, dear President, for loving the Savior so deeply. You spent your life learning of him and speaking of him. He was your best friend. You helped us become closer to our elder Brother. You understood so well Christ's atonement and the importance of the Resurrection. You became much like him. You gave hope to all of us who stumble as you gently lifted us and offered the light and the way. You provided a vital glimpse of your 'sure knowledge' when near the end you sweetly stated, 'Let's look for each other on the other side.'

"Good-bye for now, dear prophet and friend. Your Christlike qualities and goodness will be greatly missed. You are our hero. We love you forever and ever."[4]

"Remembering the Impassioned Sermon of President Ezra Taft Benson"

JON M. HUNTSMAN TO AN INDIVIDUAL
SEEKING COUNSEL
CIRCA 1995

—

Born in Blackfoot, Idaho, in 1937, Jon. M. Huntsman has served in many different Church callings, including president of the Washington, D.C., Mission, stake president, and area authority seventy. He and his wife, Karen Haight Huntsman (daughter of Elder David B. and Sister Clara Tuttle Haight), are the parents of nine children. Elder Huntsman is also a well-known businessman and philanthropist.

In an *Ensign* article on the role of the Church in Europe, Elder Russell M. Nelson of the Quorum of the Twelve discussed the Huntsmans's charitable efforts: "In June 1991, the Republic of Armenia donated land to the Church for the construction of a facility in its capital city, Yerevan, in gratitude for relief efforts extended in Armenia by the Church and its members worldwide. For example, Jon M. Huntsman, his wife, Karen, and their family have contributed funds and personal commitment to relieve thousands of homeless victims of the disastrous earthquake of December 1988. David M. Horne, a building contractor from Salt Lake City, responded to a special mission call from the Church to donate his time and skills to help build safe homes for these victims. A precast concrete fabrication facility, dedicated in Yerevan on 24 June 1991, will generate enough units to erect 6,500 apartments and provide housing for 25,000 people annually."[1]

In the following letter, sent to a woman seeking counsel, Elder Huntsman expresses his feelings on both financial and gospel principles.

—

We were deeply saddened to read of the ironic twist of fate that reversed the fortunes of your husband and his brothers, leaving you struggling with a number of troublesome economic and emotional problems. Perhaps a few observations might be helpful to you.

You wrote in your letter that there was fierce competition between your husband and his brothers. One cannot escape the parallel to the biblical story of Joseph whose brothers sold him into Egypt.* That story had a happy ending, and yours can, too.

It would not be surprising to read between the lines that in striving to maintain a now unrealistic lifestyle you have fallen into the insidious trap of consumer debt. What is surprising is the fact that so many savvy people are led to believe that if they cannot afford to buy something with cash, they will somehow be able to afford it by borrowing or buying it on credit (the same thing) and then paying off the same amount plus interest. For as long as memory serves us, our church leaders have counseled us to "get out of debt and stay out of debt" except perhaps for a home, education or medical expense.

You seem to be immobilized by the fact that your husband's brothers have prospered and are therefore able to give their children the lessons, camps and toys, while you have not yet come to terms with the fact that years ago he focused on the here and now instead of the future. There is a certain amount of denial in this.

Now, where do we go from here? Joseph took the lemon he received and made lemonade, not only for himself but for his brothers. Remembering the impassioned sermon of President Ezra Taft Benson shortly before his death citing pride† as one of our

---

*See Genesis 37–50.

†In his classic April 1989 conference address "Beware of Pride," President Benson said, "The proud make every man their adversary by pitting their intellects, opinions, works, wealth, talents, or any other worldly measuring device against others. In the words of C. S. Lewis: 'Pride gets no pleasure out of having something, only out of having more of it than the next man. . . . It is the comparison that makes you proud: the pleasure of being above the rest. Once the element of competition has gone, pride has gone.'" (Benson, "Beware of Pride," 4. The C. S. Lewis quotation is from Mere Christianity [New York: Macmillan, 1952], 109–10.)

172

greatest pitfalls, this may be a good time to swallow your pride and approach your brothers. I do not say it will be easy; it could be the most difficult thing you have ever done in your life. But it will do more for your character than anything else you could do. And it may surprise you that one or more of the brothers would have compassion and thereby learn a valuable lesson themselves. I have observed that there are quite a few of our fellow citizens who could use a little humility.

As to steps you and your family might take to turn your ship around and head it into the right direction, let me share with you a list of suggestions gleaned from published financial advisors and personal observation of hundreds of cases not unlike your own.

Please know that you and your family will be in our thoughts and prayers as you work through this difficult situation.

SUGGESTIONS FOR OVERCOMING FINANCIAL DIFFICULTIES

More and more individuals and families who succumb to the siren call of "buy now, pay later" find themselves deeply mired in debt. Ironically, a loan or gift in such circumstances can often exacerbate the problem rather than solving it. What is needed is a forthright recognition of the problem and its causes, followed by unwavering determination and self-discipline. Here are some suggestions we hope will be helpful:

1. Contact all of your creditors, explain your situation to them in all candor, and ask them to accept smaller payments over an extended period and to waive interest. They would usually prefer to do this rather than resorting to costly and unpleasant collection procedures.

2. Obtain forms from your bank or your church representatives and sit down together and list on a sheet of paper your assets and liabilities (this is called a balance sheet) and your revenues

and expenses on another sheet. In the process, determine which expenditures must be paid and which could be eliminated.

3. Resolve to live within your income. Bite the bullet. Agree that neither husband nor wife will spend a dime on anything that is not included in your budget.

4. If you have children, discuss your financial situation with them openly and seek their counsel and assistance. It is surprising how often the children have no idea as to the travail parents go through to earn the money which they give to their children for various purposes and needs. Also, children will frequently rally to the cause and help in ways not even envisioned by their parents. There is no disgrace in frugality. There is only tragedy when spending is out of control.

5. Make do. Substitute inexpensive activities for costly ones. Look for little ways to economize. If you watch the nickels, dimes and quarters, the dollars will take care of themselves. Coordinate errands in your automobiles. Disconnect the television; it is using electricity all the time it is plugged in. Television uses considerable electricity, so consider cutting down on its use. Shop for the best prices for groceries. Substitute natural grain cereals for expensive prepared cereals. Plant a vegetable garden and fruit trees. These are but a few areas for economy.

6. Restrict the use of your credit cards. Eliminate all but VISA and MasterCard, and use it only when necessary. Always pay off the full amount each month so as to avoid horrendous interest charges. If you cannot pay cash for a purchase, don't make the purchase.

7. Avoid the subtle trap of charge accounts, installment buying and so-called home equity loans which rapidly increase your debt while merely postponing the inevitable day of reckoning. Set a deadline for the elimination of all consumer debt (as opposed

to the mortgage loan you took out when you purchased your home). Adopt this simple yet profound goal: Get out of debt and stay out of debt.

8. Once you have turned the ship around, initiate a regular savings program, no matter how small at first. Learn the joy of seeing interest come your way instead of watching it drain your assets.

9. In critical cases, it is sometimes helpful to enlist the aid of a financial counselor who can help you establish better habits by overseeing all revenues and expenditures. Generally speaking there is someone in your church who would respond to a leader's request to volunteer time without charge.

—

When asked to reflect on his life, Elder Huntsman replied: "Through it all, I thank God every day for the anchor of the Church. Next to the atonement of Jesus Christ, I believe the two most important spiritual ingredients are the restoration of the gospel in its fulness and the law of consecration. This very sacred covenant represents a special blessing that permits us to give what we have to the building of the kingdom, to pay our tithes and offerings and to provide all that we have, if necessary, for the building of the Church. I think an extension of that is to help God's children wherever they may be who need help. The principle of consecration has been a great blessing in our life."[2]

Part 5

⁓

"GOOD WILL TO MEN"

FELLOWSHIP
WITH PUBLIC
FIGURES

"The Angel Appeared . . . Three Times the Same Night"

JOSEPH SMITH TO JOHN WENTWORTH
1 MARCH 1842

During the fall and winter of 1841–42, Joseph and Emma Smith faced sorrows that were all too typical throughout their seventeen-year marriage. On 25 August 1841, Joseph's younger brother Don Carlos died of malaria* at age twenty-five, leaving a widow, and three daughters under the age of six. Joseph and Emma's fifteen-month-old baby, named after Don Carlos, also caught malaria, and died on 15 September. This was the fifth infant Joseph and Emma had lost (including their adopted son Joseph Murdock). Baby Don Carols's death proved a particular trial for Emma, pregnant and in poor health herself. Two weeks later, Hyrum's second son also died of malaria.

Winter brought more deaths. Samuel Smith's wife, Mary Bailey Smith, and infant daughter died on 25 January 1842, at a time when Emma was help-ing to care for an ill Lucy Mack Smith. On 6 February, Emma gave birth to another boy, but the baby did not survive. Ten days later Emma's mother, Elizabeth Lewis, whom Emma probably had not seen for eleven years, died at age seventy-four.†

But the coming spring in beautiful Nauvoo brought new hope. The Saints were relatively free from persecution, and Joseph and Emma took joy in their young family of one daughter and three sons, ranging in age from four to eleven. Then Joseph talked to friends William and Anna McIntire, who had

---

*"The summer heat [in Nauvoo] brought mosquitoes and with them the fever and chills of malaria." (Newell and Avery, 102.)

†According to the Wells, Vermont, town record, Elizabeth Lewis was born on 19 November 1767. Twenty years later, Oliver Cowdery's parents, William Cowdery and Rebecca Fuller, moved to Wells. Oliver was born there in 1806. Since Isaac Hale (Emma's father) and Elizabeth Lewis and the Cowderys were all in Wells in the late 1780s, it is possible they knew each other. Isaac Hale and Elizabeth Lewis were married in 1790. Within a year they had settled in Pennsylvania near the Susquehanna River.

been blessed with twin girls three months earlier. To comfort Emma, Joseph arranged to bring one of the twin girls for Emma to nurse each day and then returned the baby to her parents each night.*

The tranquil evening of Wednesday, 9 March found Joseph and Emma together in Joseph's office, both involved in historic projects. Joseph translated and revised parts of the Book of Abraham (which was published in March and May of 1842), and Emma very likely prepared for the first meeting of the new women's benevolent society.†

It was during this peaceful period‡ that Joseph, thirty-six, wrote a 2,800-word missive to John Wentworth,§ twenty-six. It would become the most famous letter in the history of the Church.**

———

I was born in the town of Sharon Windsor co., Vermont, on the 23d of December, A. D. 1805. When ten years old my parents

———

*"When the child died at age two, both Emma and Joseph grieved with her parents." (Newell and Avery, 104.)

†Joseph's record for the day reads as follows: "Wednesday, 9.—Examining copy for the *Times and Seasons*, presented by Messrs. Taylor and Bennett, and a variety of other business in my office, in the morning; in the afternoon continued the translation of the Book of Abraham, called at Bishop Knight's and Mr. Davis,' with the recorder, and continued translating and revising, and reading letters in the evening, Sister Emma being present in the office." (*HC*, 4:548.) Joseph was also sealed polygynously to Patty Bartlett Sessions on 9 March. (Faulring, *An American Prophet's Record*, xxxi.) The Relief Society was officially organized on 17 March 1842.

‡The peace was short lived. On 8 August 1842, Joseph was arrested for complicity in an assassination attempt on Missouri Governor Lilburn W. Boggs. Joseph went into hiding. He later gave himself up and was acquitted.

§"John Wentworth (1815–88) was born at Sandwich, Carroll County, New York. Soon after his graduation from Dartmouth College, in 1836, he became editor of the weekly paper *Chicago Democrat*, and after three years became its owner. He was elected to the United States House of Representatives in 1843, serving six terms in Congress. In 1857 he was elected mayor of Chicago. He died at Chicago, Cook County, Illinois." (Vogel, *Early Mormon Documents*, 1:169.)

**Dan Vogel suggests that Joseph relied on Orson Pratt's *An Interesting Account of Several Remarkable Visions and of the Late Discovery of Ancient American Records* in preparing the Wentworth letter. (*Early Mormon Documents*, 1:169.)

removed to Palmyra New York, where we resided about four years, and from thence we removed to the town of Manchester.

My father was a farmer and taught me the art of husbandry. When about fourteen years of age I began to reflect upon the importance of being prepared for a future state, and upon enquiring the plan of salvation I found that there was a great clash in religious sentiment; if I went to one society they referred me to one plan, and another to another; each one pointing to his own particular creed as the summum bonum of perfection: considering that all could not be right, and that God could not be the author of so much confusion I determined to investigate the subject more fully, believing that if God had a church it would not be split up into factions, and that if he taught one society to worship one way, and administer in one set of ordinances, he would not teach another principles which were diametrically opposed. Believing the word of God I had confidence in the declaration of James: "If any man lack wisdom let him ask of God who giveth to all men liberally and upbraideth not and it shall be given him," I retired to a secret place in a grove and began to call upon the Lord, while fervently engaged in supplication my mind was taken away from the objects with which I was surrounded, and I was enwrapped in a heavenly vision and saw two glorious personages who exactly resembled each other in features, and likeness, surrounded with a brilliant light which eclipsed the sun at noon-day. They told me that all religious denominations were believing in incorrect doctrines, and that none of them was acknowledged of God as his church and kingdom. And I was expressly commanded to "go not after them," at the same time receiving a promise that the fulness of the gospel should at some future time be made known unto me.

On the evening of the 21st of September, A. D. 1823, while I was praying unto God, and endeavoring to exercise faith in the precious promises of scripture on a sudden a light like that of day, only of a far purer and more glorious appearance, and brightness burst into the room, indeed the first sight was as though the house was filled with consuming fire; the appearance produced a shock that affected the whole body; in a moment a personage stood before me surrounded with a glory yet greater than that with which I was already surrounded. This messenger proclaimed himself to be an angel of God sent to bring the joyful tidings, that the covenant which God made with ancient Israel was at hand to be fulfilled, that the preparatory work for the second coming of the Messiah was speedily to commence; that the time was at hand for the gospel, in all its fulness to be preached in power, unto all nations that a people might be prepared for the millennial reign.

I was informed that I was chosen to be an instrument in the hands of God to bring about some of his purposes in this glorious dispensation.

I was also informed concerning the aboriginal inhabitants of this country, and shown who they were, and from whence they came; a brief sketch of their origin, progress, civilization, laws, governments, of their righteousness and iniquity, and the blessings of God being finally withdrawn from them as a people was made known unto me: I was also told where there was deposited some plates on which were engraven an abridgement of the records of the ancient prophets that had existed on this continent. The angel appeared to me three times the same night and unfolded the same things. After having received many visits from the angels of God unfolding the majesty, and glory of the events that should transpire in the last days, on the morning of the 22d of September A. D. 1827, the angel of the Lord delivered the records into my hands.

These records were engraven on plates which had the appearance of gold, each plate was six inches wide and eight inches long and not quite so thick as common tin. They were filled with engravings, in Egyptian characters and bound together in a volume, as the leaves of a book with three rings running through the whole. The volume was something near six inches in thickness, a part of which was sealed. The characters on the unsealed part were small, and beautifully engraved. The whole book exhibited many marks of antiquity in its construction and much skill in the art of engraving. With the records was found a curious instrument which the ancients called "Urim and Thummim," which consisted of two transparent stones set in the rim of a bow fastened to a breastplate.

Through the medium of the Urim and Thummim I translated the record by the gift, and power of God.

In this important and interesting book the history of ancient America is unfolded, from its first settlement by a colony that came from the tower of Babel, at the confusion of languages to the beginning of the fifth century of the Christian era. We are informed by these records that America in ancient times has been inhabited by two distinct races of people. The first were called Jaredites and came directly from the tower of Babel. The second race came directly from the city of Jerusalem, about six hundred years before Christ. They were principally Israelites, of the descendants of Joseph. The Jaredites were destroyed about the time that the Israelites came from Jerusalem, who succeeded them in the inheritance of the country. The principal nation of the second race fell in battle towards the close of the fourth century. The remnant are the Indians that now inhabit this country. This book also tells us that our Saviour made his appearance upon this continent after his resurrection, that he planted the gospel here in all its fulness, and richness, and power, and blessing; that they had apostles, prophets, pastors, teachers and evangelists; the same order, the same priesthood, the same ordinances, gifts, powers, and blessing, as was enjoyed on the eastern continent, that the people were cut off in consequence of their transgressions, that the last of their prophets who existed among them was commanded to write an abridgement of their prophesies, history &c., and to hide it up in the earth, and that it should come forth and be united with the bible for the accomplishment of the purposes of God in the last days. For a more particular account I would refer to the Book of Mormon, which can be purchased at Nauvoo, or from any of our travelling elders.

As soon as the news of this discovery was made known, false reports, misrepresentation and slander flew as on the wings of the wind in every direction, the house was frequently beset by mobs, and evil designing persons, several times I was shot at, and very narrowly escaped, and every device was made use of to get the plates away from me, but the power and blessing of God attended me, and several began to believe my testimony.

On the 6th of April, 1830, the "Church of Jesus Christ of Latter-Day Saints," was first organized in the town of Manchester, Ontario co., state of New York. Some few were called and ordained by the spirit of revelation, and prophesy, and began to preach as the spirit gave them utterance, and though weak, yet were they strengthened by the power of God, and many were brought to repentance, were immersed in the water, and were filled with the Holy Ghost by the laying on of hands. They saw visions and prophesied, devils were cast out and the sick healed by the laying on of hands. From that time the work rolled forth with astonishing rapidity, and churches were soon formed in the states of New York, Pennsylvania, Ohio, Indiana, Illinois and Missouri;

in the last named state a considerable settlement was formed in Jackson co.; numbers joined the church and we were increasing rapidly; we made large purchases of land, our farms teemed with plenty, and peace and happiness was enjoyed in our domestic circle and throughout our neighborhood; but as we could not associate with our neighbors who were many of them of the basest of men and had fled from the face of civilized society, to the frontier country to escape the hand of justice, in their midnight revels, their sabbath breaking, horseracing, and gambling, they commenced at first ridicule, then to persecute, and finally an organized mob assembled and burned our houses, tarred, and feathered, and whipped many of our brethren and finally drove them from their habitations; who houseless, and homeless, contrary to law, justice and humanity, had to wander on the bleak prairies till the children left the tracks of their blood on the prairie, this took place in the month of November, and they had no other covering but the canopy of heaven, in this inclement season of the year; this proceeding was winked at by the government and although we had warrantee deeds for our land, and had violated no law we could obtain no redress.

There were many sick, who were thus inhumanly driven from their houses, and had to endure all this abuse and to seek homes where they could be found. The result was, that a great many of them being deprived of the comforts of life, and the necessary attendances, died; many children were left orphans; wives, widows; and husbands widowers.—Our farms were taken possession of by the mob, many thousands of cattle, sheep, horses, and hogs, were taken and our household goods, store goods, and printing press, and type were broken, taken, or otherwise destroyed.

Many of our brethren removed to Clay where they continued until 1836, three years; there was no violence offered but there were threatnings of violence. But in the summer of 1836, these threatnings began to assume a more serious form; from threats, public meetings were called, resolutions were passed, vengeance and destruction were threatened, and affairs again assumed a fearful attitude, Jackson county was a sufficient precedent, and as the authorities in that county did not interfere, they boasted that they would not in this, which on application to the authorities we found to be too true, and after much violence, privation and loss of property we were again driven from our homes.

We next settled in Caldwell, and Davies counties, where we made large and extensive settlements, thinking to free ourselves from the power of oppression, by settling in new counties, with very few inhabitants in them; but here we were not allowed to live in peace, but in 1838 we were again attacked by mobs an exterminating order was issued by Gov. Boggs, and under the sanction of law an organized banditti ranged through the country, robbed us of our cattle, sheep, horses, hogs &c., many of our people were murdered in cold blood, the chastity of our women was violated, and we were forced to sign away our property at the point of the sword, and after enduring every indignity that could be heaped upon us by an inhuman, ungodly band of maurauders, from twelve to fifteen thousand souls men, women, and children were driven from their own fire sides, and from lands that they had warrantee deeds of, houseless, friendless, and homeless (in the depth of winter,) to wander as exiles on the earth or to seek an asylum in a more genial clime, and among a less barbarous people.

Many sickened and died, in consequence of the cold, and hardships they had to endure; many wives were left widows, and children orphans, and destitute. It would take more time than is allotted me here to describe the injustice, the wrongs, the murders, the bloodshed, the theft, misery and woe that has been caused by the barbarous, inhuman, and lawless, proceedings of the state of Missouri.

In the situation before alluded to we arrived in the state of Illinois in 1839, where we found a hospitable people and a friendly home; a people who were willing to be governed by the principles of law and humanity. We have commenced to build a city called "Nauvoo" in Hancock co., we number from six to eight thousand here besides vast numbers in the county around and in almost every county of the state. We have a city charter granted us and a charter for a legion the troops of which now number 1500. We have also a charter for a university, for an agricultural and manufacturing society, have our own laws and administrators, and possess all the privileges that other free and enlightened citizens enjoy.

Persecution has not stopped the progress of truth, but has only added fuel to the flame, it has spread with increasing rapidity, proud of the cause which they have espoused and conscious of their innocence and of the truth of their system amidst calumny and reproach have the elders of this church gone forth, and planted the gospel in almost every state in the Union; it has penetrated our cities, it has spread over our villages, and has caused thousands of our intelligent, noble, and patriotic citizens to obey its divine mandates, and be governed by its sacred truths. It has also spread into England, Ireland, Scotland and Wales: in the year of 1839 where a few of our missionaries were sent over five thousand joined the standard of truth, there are numbers now joining in every land.

Our missionaries are going forth to different nations, and in Germany, Palestine, New Holland, the East Indies, and other places, the standard of truth has been erected: no unhallowed hand can stop the work from progressing, persecutions may rage, mobs may combine, armies may assemble, calumny may defame, but the truth of God will go forth boldly, nobly, and independent till it has penetrated every continent, visited every clime, swept every country, and sounded in every ear, till the purposes of God shall be accomplished and the great Jehovah shall say the work is done.

We believe in God the Eternal Father, and in his son Jesus Christ, and in the Holy Ghost.

We believe that men will be punished for their own sins and not for Adam's transgression.

We believe that through the atonement of Christ all mankind may be saved by obedience to the laws and ordinances of the Gospel.

We believe that these ordinances are 1st, Faith in the Lord Jesus Christ; 2d, Repentance; 3d, Baptism by immersion for the remission of sins; 4th, Laying on of hands for the gift of the Holy Ghost.

We believe that a man must be called of God by "prophesy, and by laying on of hands" by those who are in authority to preach the gospel and administer in the ordinances thereof.

We believe in the same organization that existed in the primitive church, viz: apostles, prophets, pastors, teachers, evangelists &c.

We believe in the gift of tongues, prophesy, revelation, visions, healing, interpretation of tongues &c.

We believe the bible to be the word of God as far as it is translated correctly; we also believe the Book of Mormon to be the word of God.

We believe all that God has revealed, all that he does now

reveal, and we believe that he will yet reveal many great and important things pertaining to the kingdom of God.

We believe in the literal gathering of Israel and in the restoration of the Ten Tribes. That Zion will be built upon this continent. That Christ will reign personally upon the earth, and that the earth will be renewed and receive its paradasaic glory.

We claim the privilege of worshipping Almighty God according to the dictates of our conscience, and allow all men the same privilege let them worship how, where, or what they may.

We believe in being subject to kings, presidents, rulers, and magistrates, in obeying, honoring and sustaining the law.

We believe in being honest, true, chaste, benevolent, virtuous, and in doing good to *all men*; indeed we may say that we follow the admonition of Paul "we believe all things we hope all things," we have endured many things and hope to be able to endure all things. If there is any thing virtuous, lovely, or of good report or praise worthy we seek after these things. Respectfully &c.,

JOSEPH SMITH.

B. H. Roberts aptly summed up the significance of this document when he wrote that an important account of the First Vision "is found in what is called the *Wentworth Letter*, which was written to Mr. John Wentworth, editor and proprietor of the *Chicago Democrat*, at the latter's solicitation, as he wished to present the Prophet's statement of the origin and progress of "Mormonism" to his friend, a Mr. Bastow* who was then writing a history of New Hampshire. The letter is one of the choicest documents in our church literature; as also it is the earliest published document by the Prophet

---

*The correct name is George Barstow, according to Vogel.

personally, making any pretension to consecutive narrative of those events in which the great Latter-day work had its origin. . . . Referring again to this *Wentworth Letter*, I may say that for combining conciseness of statement with comprehensiveness of treatment of the subject with which it deals, it has few equals among historical documents, and certainly none that excel it in our church literature. In it one has in a few pages (less than six of these pages) a remarkably clear statement of the leading events in the church history up to that time, and an epitome of her doctrines, from the beginning—the birth of the Prophet, in 1805—up to the date of publication, March, 1842, a period of thirty-six years."[1]

"The Report Is Utterly False"

REED SMOOT TO THEODORE ROOSEVELT
27 MAY 1904

When LDS Apostle and businessman Reed Smoot ran for the U.S. Senate in 1902, in the midst of a national furor over plural marriage, opposition arose from many quarters. In Utah, the Salt Lake Ministerial Association drafted a resolution urging Smoot's defeat and sent it to Theodore Roosevelt, who had assumed the presidency after William McKinley's assassination in September of 1901. Roosevelt suggested that it would be advisable for Smoot to drop out of the race.

The fiercely independent Roosevelt soon had second thoughts, however. Reed's good friend and business partner—and nonmember of the Church— C. E. Loose later reported that he spent an hour with Roosevelt before the election.

"Is Smoot a polygamist?" Roosevelt asked.

"No," came the reply.

"Are Mormons good Americans?"

"Yes, and I know because I know them," answered Loose.[1]

When the Utah state legislature elected Smoot in 1903, a national controversy erupted. From 1904 to 1906, a Senate committee held hearings to determine if Smoot should be allowed to keep his seat. "Smoot's right to hold office was challenged on two grounds: first, that he and other Church leaders continued to teach plural marriage, even if he did not practice it; and second, that the First Presidency and the Quorum of the Twelve Apostles, not the republic, would have first claim on his loyalties."[2]

When Smoot saw fellow Republican Roosevelt later in 1903, the president expressed concern over Utah's vote in the upcoming 1904 presidential election (Utah had voted Republican in the 1900 election). Smoot was able to reassure him. "Mr. Smoot," said the president, "you are a good enough American, or Gentile for that matter, for me."[3]

Senator Smoot and President Roosevelt thus became allies, which was no small factor in Smoot's retaining his seat in the Senate.* The following exchange of letters demonstrates the goodwill that existed between the two men. Reed Smoot was forty-two and Teddy Roosevelt forty-five when they wrote these letters.

———

Provo City, Utah, May 27, 1904
Honorable Theordore Roosevelt,
Washington, D. C.
Mr. President:

I delivered an address on my return home before the Ladies' Republican Club of Provo City, and the next morning the Salt Lake Herald, in its report of my remarks, stated that I made the following statement:

"I am proud to say that Roosevelt will not carry New York."

From press clippings I have received, I notice that this statement is attributed to me by a great many of the leading papers of the country. It has been copied as being true, and comments made upon it, and, perhaps, it has come to your notice. I assure you it is utterly false. It was published for the purpose of hurting

_____

*Theodore Roosevelt's friendship with the Church began as early as 1900, when he was campaigning for vice president. At a campaign stop in Rexburg, Idaho, prominent Church leader Ben E. Rich introduced Roosevelt and praised him, even predicting that he would one day be president. The comments impressed Roosevelt, and two years later, when he was president, he spotted Rich in the crowd as he was riding in a parade in Chattanooga, Tennessee. Roosevelt stopped the procession and walked over and shook hands with President Rich, then president of the Southern States Mission. After they talked briefly, Roosevelt said, "I think now by this recognition, you will have more friends in the South." (Benjamin L. Rich, *Ben E. Rich: An Appreciation by His Son*. Salt Lake City: N.p. 1950; cited in Garr, Cannon, and Cowan, 1044.) In 1911, Roosevelt published a letter in *Collier's* magazine that defended the Church against spurious attacks.

me with the party leaders and you with the voters of Utah and perhaps with the voters of other states. The following is the substance of what I did say:

There is a great deal of talk in the East about President Roosevelt not being able to carry New York, and the only reason given is that the trusts and great money interests are opposed to him. If he should lose New York by such opposition, I am sure the American people would be proud of him as a president who was not afraid to do his duty. He will be elected the next president of the United States without doubt, even if New York does vote against him.

Excuse me for bringing this to your attention, but I felt that it was due me to let you know that the report is false.

With kind personal regards, and best wishes, I remain

Yours sincerely

A President's Kind Reply

THEODORE ROOSEVELT TO REED SMOOT
2 JUNE 1904

June 2, 1904.

Dear Senator:

I had not seen that report, but if I had I should have known that it was false. I thank you for writing me.

Sincerely yours,

Theodore Roosevelt

Hon. Reed Smoot,

Provo City, Utah.

Teddy Roosevelt, who had achieved renown as a writer, adventurer, and war hero before becoming the youngest U.S. president in history, proved to be quite popular. In 1904 he carried both Utah and New York, as well as all other states in the West, Midwest, and East, losing only in the South. He won 56 percent of the popular vote; his opponent, Alton B. Parker, received 38 percent. Though he probably could have won the 1908 election as well, Roosevelt stepped down, but not before hand picking his successor, William Howard Taft.

Characteristically, Roosevelt then traveled to Africa for a safari and nature study, followed by a grand tour of European cities. But by 1910 he was back in the United States and deeply concerned about the future of the Republican Party. He eventually opposed Taft and ran against him in the 1912 primaries. When the convention nominated Taft, Roosevelt formed the Progressive Party. He was campaigning in Milwaukee, Wisconsin, when a would-be assassin shot him. Roosevelt, the "Rough Rider," recovered, saying it took more than that to kill a "bull moose," a phrase used from that time to describe the Progressives. But with the traditional Republican vote split between Taft and Roosevelt, Democrat Woodrow Wilson won the 1912 election by a large margin, with Roosevelt placing second.

Roosevelt contracted tropical fever on an expedition to Brazil in 1914, and his health declined over the next few years. He supported U.S. involvement in World War I, and all four of his sons fought in the war. In August 1918, just two months before the Armistice, Roosevelt's youngest son, Quentin, was killed in action. Suffering from these personal and political losses, Teddy Roosevelt died of a blood clot on 6 January 1919 at his home in Sagamore Hill, Oyster Bay, New York. He was sixty years old.

Apostle Reed Smoot, whose political career had been so uncertain at one point, served for thirty years, becoming one of the most powerful and respected men in the Senate. His influence helped the Church reestablish a missionary program in Europe after World War I, and he was able to dispel many myths about Mormonism.

Ironically, just as a Roosevelt had helped Reed Smoot secure his Senate seat, another Roosevelt—Franklin Delano, whose father was a cousin to Teddy—was instrumental in his downfall. When Democrat FDR handily defeated Republican Herbert Hoover in 1932, a number of Republican Senators were also swept out of office, Reed Smoot among them. Smoot took the defeat quite personally. Although he continued his apostolic duties, his life seemed to him anticlimactic in many ways.

"After my mission I came to know Reed Smoot," Hugh B. Brown later wrote. "He was quite a fearless man. . . . He was a great representative of the people of Utah and of the church. . . . [His defeat in 1932] was a terrible shock to him, and I do not know that he ever really overcame the impact during his lifetime. . . . I talked to him on the golf course shortly before his death in 1941.

"'I know that what has happened to me is not the result of my church or my standing in the church,' he said, 'but because of some astute politicians who through the years have determined to get me and now it seems some members of the church (since Brother [Elbert] Thomas [who defeated Smoot in the Senate race] was then a member of the General Board of the Sunday School) have seemed to turn against me. For sometime I held it against them, but I think now I understand that it was the usual course of political activity, and that I had served the time that I was expected to serve.'"[4]

"We Are in for a Ten Years' War"

HERBERT HOOVER TO J. REUBEN CLARK JR.
13 NOVEMBER 1941

For two-and-a-half decades prior to his call to the First Presidency in 1933, J. Reuben Clark Jr. had served in a variety of prominent positions in the U.S. State Department, including solicitor, special counsel, and under secretary of state. Herbert Hoover was also prominent in Washington, D.C., during this period, serving as commissioner for relief in Belgium, United States food administrator, and secretary of commerce.

A brilliant engineer as a young man, Herbert Hoover had become wealthy in his thirties; after that time he devoted his time to public service, often donating his salary to charity. He was in London in 1914, when World War I broke out, and at the request of U.S. officials there, he organized a committee that assisted more than 100,000 U.S. citizens in returning home. He then established the commission for relief in Belgium to assist victims of the war in that country. From 1914 to 1917 he directed the effort to collect and distribute food, saving thousands of lives in the process.

Hoover was elected president of the United States in 1928; two years later he appointed J. Reuben Clark Jr. ambassador to Mexico. The two men shared views on a number of political issues and corresponded over the years. After World War II erupted in Europe in 1939, both of them opposed U.S. involvement in the war. In August of 1941, they joined fourteen other prominent Republicans in a strongly worded statement urging Congress to stop preparations for an undeclared war. Two months after that, Hoover, sixty-seven, sent the following letter to President Clark, seventy, then first counselor to Heber J. Grant (with David O. McKay as second counselor).

The Waldorf-Astoria Towers

New York City

November 13, 1941

My dear Reuben:

I am making what I hope is the strongest speech of my life on "Shall We Send Armies to Europe?" before the Union League Club of Chicago on Wednesday, November 19th. It will be broadcast over Columbia Broadcasting System from 10:15 to 10:45 Eastern Standard Time, 9:15 to 9:45 Central Standard Time, 8:15 to 8:45 Mountain Standard Time, 7:15 to 7:45 Pacific Standard Time. I am convinced this is the next Administration move, and unless it be checked we are in for a ten years' war.

It is difficult these days to get the Press Associations to carry notice of such speeches, and often enough the local broadcasting stations do not accept it. I am wondering, therefore, in the common interest, if you or through friends would check up to see that the local Columbia station carries it, and if you or through friends would see that notice of the speech is given in the Press thereabouts.

Yours faithfully,

Herbert Hoover

Mr. J. Reuben Clark, Jr.

47 East South Temple Street

Salt Lake City, Utah

President Clark immediately responded with a telegram that read, "KSL will carry broadcast on nineteenth. If you will send copy will see it is printed. Best wishes for your success."[1] Three weeks later, however, on Sunday, 7 December 1941, Japanese forces attacked Pearl Harbor, and the United States was thrust into the war. Hoover acknowledged that the United States had to defend itself but did not believe that defense should involve becoming allies with the Soviet Union.

President Clark, who had lost a son-in-law at Pearl Harbor, continued to oppose U.S. involvement in the struggle and after the war criticized Allied bombings in Germany and Japan.* He also opposed a "great standing army" and a peacetime draft.[2]

J. Reuben Clark and Herbert Hoover continued to correspond during their long, productive lives. They both died at age ninety, President Clark in 1961 and President Hoover in 1964.

---

*For example, President Clark stated at the October 1946 general conference: "Now do not forget that all of the nations had prepared before World War II to use aircraft; they had already used submarines in World War I; and we in this area know we were prepared to use poison gases. Then as the crowning savagery of the war, we Americans wiped out hundreds of thousands of civilian population with the atom bomb in Japan, few if any of the ordinary civilians being any more responsible for the war than were we, and perhaps most of them no more aiding Japan in the war than we were aiding America. Military men are now saying that the atom bomb was a mistake. It was more than that: it was a world tragedy. Thus we have lost all that we gained during the years from Grotius (1625) to 1912. And the worst of this atomic bomb tragedy is not that not only did the people of the United States not rise up in protest against this savagery, not only did it not shock us to read of this wholesale destruction of men, women, and children, and cripples, but that it actually drew from the nation at large a general approval of this fiendish butchery." (Conference Report, October 1946, 89.)

"Sam Cowley Had True Courage"

J. EDGAR HOOVER TO J. WILLARD MARRIOTT
7 MAY 1958

—

When prominent LDS businessman and Church leader J. Willard Marriott requested information from J. Edgar Hoover* concerning LDS FBI agents, Hoover responded with the following highly complimentary letter and statement. In the statement, Hoover gives a detailed history of the FBI career of Samuel P. Cowley, who was the son of Apostle Matthias F. Cowley and half-brother of Apostle Matthew Cowley. Samuel Parkinson Cowley was born 23 July 1899 (two years after Matthew Cowley) and died 28 November 1934. (His mother was Luella Smart Parkinson; Matthew's mother was Abigail Hyde.) Interestingly, Hoover also mentions the son of another apostle, Paul John Callis, the son of Apostle Charles A. Callis and Grace Pack. Paul John Callis was born 12 December 1912 and died in Ely, Nevada, 2 November 1957.

J. Edgar Hoover was sixty-three when he wrote the following letter to J. Willard Marriott, fifty-seven:

—

May 7, 1958
Mr. J. Willard Marriott
4500 Garfield Street, Northwest
Washington, D.C.

---

*J. Edgar Hoover was born 1 January 1895 and died 2 May 1972. He served as director of the FBI from 1924 until his death forty-eight years later. He was a highly controversial figure both during his lifetime and afterwards. During his time as director, the FBI captured many notorious criminals and broke up several spy rings. Yet it also was accused of violating the civil rights of many people it investigated and of using investigations for political favor. Hoover's personal life is also a matter of controversy.

Dear Mr. Marriott:

In line with your telephonic request of May 1, there is enclosed a statement regarding members of your church employed by the FBI whose habits and standards of conduct have come to my attention. It was a pleasure to be of service in this matter, and I do hope the enclosed material will suit your needs.

Sincerely yours,

J. Edgar Hoover

Enclosure

Washington, D.C.

May 7, 1958

STATEMENT OF JOHN EDGAR HOOVER
DIRECTOR, FEDERAL BUREAU OF INVESTIGATION
FURNISHED TO J. WILLARD MARRIOTT

One of the first things which a visitor sees when he enters my reception room in the FBI is a bronze plaque. This plaque bears the names of Service Martyrs—men who have been killed in [the] line of duty. Among the names on the plaque appears that of Samuel P. Cowley,* Inspector in the FBI. A picture of Sam hangs on the wall of the same room. When I think of such words as "courage," "honor," and "dependability," the name of Sam Cowley and the face in the picture come first to mind. I have said many times that Sam Cowley was the bravest man I ever knew. That belief is based on something more than the knowledge that he had the physical and mental fortitude to go out and face kill-crazy gangsters whose false courage lasted only while they had lead in their guns.

---

*In the October 1952 *Improvement Era*, Hoover and coauthor Ken Jones published an extensive article about Samuel P. Cowley.

Sam Cowley had true courage. He was a plain, direct, devout man with the simplicity of true worth, honor and dignity. His whole life was based on simple faith and determination to do his duty. What was necessary to do was done with dignity.

There was no pretentiousness in Sam Cowley. No honest labor was beneath his dignity. He worked to achieve his education. During the summer months of 1921 through 1924, Sam sold knit goods. In the winter he went to school. He worked briefly in a department store, then in another Government Agency before, in 1929, he entered the Department of Justice as a Special Agent in the Division of Investigation, now known as the FBI.

We soon found that Special Agent Cowley was a man who turned out a large volume of work and who accepted responsibility and asked for more. His attitude was commendable, his loyalty beyond question, and his personal habits were above reproach. One supervisor said of him, "The longer one knows him the more you realize his true worth." Another said, "He voluntarily works too much," and "He has a habit of consistently doing things right."

It was intelligent persistence and his thoroughness in doing what needed to be done which propelled Special Agent Cowley into his executive position. Once he wrote in a brief note after he had received a well-earned raise in salary:

"I appreciate this advancement . . . but more so, because of the fact that it indicates to me that you have seen fit to place additional responsibility and confidence in me. I hope that you will not be disappointed in my efforts to contribute to the splendid work being performed. . . . I am enjoying more than I can express my work here . . . the more responsibility, the more I enjoy it."

From the beginning, Special Agent Cowley was a man who

lived his work. He served his investigative apprenticeship in various Division offices where his abilities became so manifest that he was called in to the Seat of Government at Washington, D.C., to fill an executive position. He rose rapidly through various executive offices until at the time of his death he held the position of Inspector and had to his credit the solution of highly important cases. Inspector Cowley had been placed on special assignment in certain vital investigations. He was in full charge of all investigative activity directed toward the location and apprehension of gangster John Dillinger. That assignment was brought to an effective conclusion. He was assigned to the supervision of the Bremer kidnapping case and the Kansas City Massacre investigations. He was the Inspector in Charge of Special Agents seeking to apprehend Lester Gillis, alias "Baby Face" Nelson.

Sam Cowley served with us for barely five years. On November 24, 1934, he and a fellow Agent encountered John Paul Chase and infamous killer Lester Gillis and the latter's wife, near Barrington, Illinois. In the gun battle which followed, Gillis, who had previously murdered a Special Agent and wounded another, was shot and fatally wounded. Agent Herman Hollis was killed instantly, and Sam Cowley received wounds which resulted in his death. But even as he lay there injured he urged the officer who came to his aid to take care of his companion first.

One wonders what makes such a man as Sam Cowley. I think one of my co-workers found the answer. This man said that Sam never spoke to him about matters of religion, but that his attitude and bearing were those of a man whose faith was rooted in certain basic certainties and who knew that results were beyond human responsibility and power. "His was the calm of a man who did his best and left the final decision to a Higher Power."

Sam was deeply and devoutly religious—a man of great faith.

As a member of the Church of Jesus Christ of Latter Day Saints, Sam, from 1916 until 1920, did missionary work in the Hawaiian Islands. Later, despite his extremely heavy schedule, Sam served his church in the capacity of Sunday School teacher.

The longer I live the more certain I become that faith is the source of strength which enables men to hold to their duty in the face of overwhelming odds. I am just as certain that faith is the sustaining fact which holds men to the monotonous but necessary tasks which go into making up so much of living. Good law enforcement requires men of faith.

There is a plaque at Sam Cowley's school in Utah which says that he "died in the service of his country November 28, 1934, for the cause of justice and the safety of his fellow men."

I am proud of the fact that the FBI can boast that there are many Special Agents and other employees of Sam's religious affiliation who are living in the service of their country. It is a well known fact that the Mormon religion places great emphasis on self-discipline. That fact, I am sure, helps account for many of the statements which are revealed to us in the course of investigating applicants. Such remarks as: "Honesty and integrity beyond question," "Young man of excellent character and habits," and "Fine young man of excellent qualities" appear often. Who can deny that the training afforded in the home and the church is largely responsible?

While I have no way of knowing how many of our personnel are members of the Church of Jesus Christ of Latter Day Saints, inasmuch as no record of the religious affiliations of FBI employees is maintained, I have in the course of events and through personal acquaintance learned something of the religious background of some employees. I know that some members of the Mormon faith have risen to high executive positions. W. Cleon

Skousen, presently Chief of Police at Salt Lake City, Utah, was a most effective administrator at the Seat of Government, as well as a fine lecturer and teacher in police schools. Mr. Skousen, who spent two years as a student missionary for his church in the British Isles, continued to take an active role in his church despite his heavy schedule or work in the FBI. It was, indeed, in part because of religious obligations that he resigned to accept an important post in a Mormon institution of higher learning. His active interest in the field of prevention of juvenile delinquency is well known. Only recently his book emphasizing the menace of communism was published.

The Special Agent in Charge of one of our west coast offices was reared in the Mormon faith. The assistant special agent in charge of another western office is a member of the same faith. Another agent, whose administrative and executive ability in personnel work has earned him a highly responsible position supervising approximately seven hundred employees, certainly must be counted as among those holding vital positions. This man's work demands infinite attention to detail as well as a broad understanding of people. Despite his heavy responsibilities, this supervisor continues to take an active part in the life of his church.

That busy men find time for spiritual duties was again emphasized in the life of the Resident Agent at Reno, Nevada, who was killed last fall in a tragic automobile accident. Special Agent Paul Callis was a leader of the Mormon Church in Reno. At the time of his death in November, 1957, Mr. Callis was president of the Reno Stake.

The habits and standards of personnel other than Special Agents of the FBI are also vital to the operation of our organization. We strive to find young people of integrity to man the many clerical positions in the FBI. We find that those who have a basic faith are those who stand up best in the face of disastrous odds. This is exemplified in the experience of a youthful employee who came to us from Arizona in 1948 as a clerk in the Identification Division. He was an active member of the Mormon Church. His father was dead and it was necessary that he work to help support the family. In 1950, when only twenty-one, this young man suffered a broken neck in a swimming accident in Chesapeake Bay with resultant paralysis. He was given only twenty-four hours to live, but the will to live triumphed and tremendous faith and superb courage helped that young man fight his way back on the long road of rehabilitation to effective living. We who were inspired by the splendid courage and faith which kept his morale high have tried to keep in touch with him. Two years ago we were thrilled to note that this young man of faith was chosen as the outstanding 1956 physically handicapped employee in the Phoenix, Arizona, area.

Courage, in the face of blazing guns or shocking disaster, like the courage required to do one's best in the discharge of daily duties, springs from the fountain of faith. And that fountain is kept alive and is fed through the practice of religion.

"You Have Gained an Indelible Place in History"

G. HOMER DURHAM TO BARRY GOLDWATER
28 MAY 1976

———

G. Homer Durham, who was ordained a member of the First Quorum of the Seventy in 1977, served as president of Arizona State University during the 1960s and got to know Senator Barry Goldwater well. Goldwater, a Republican who ran unsuccessfully for U.S. president in 1964, was also friendly with such Church members as Ernest L. Wilkinson, president of BYU, and Ezra Taft Benson. (However, George Romney, prominent Church member and a more moderate Republican, was not enthusiastic about Goldwater's candidacy.*)

Barry Goldwater was born in Arizona in 1909, before it became a state, and grew up there, where he had favorable impressions of the Mormon pioneers who had colonized the area. As his 1964 campaign wound to a stop, he gave his last speech in the small Mormon community of Fredonia, Arizona.

The elder statesman Barry Goldwater revealed a personal side when he wrote: "No words are adequate to describe one loss in my life—the passing of my beloved wife, Peggy, who died on December 11, 1985. We were married for fifty-one years. My life and home have been empty without her.

"I still listen for her voice. When I do not hear it, I often look beyond the hills of our valley to where she's patiently waiting for me—as she faithfully did for so many years of our married life."[1]

G. Homer Durham was sixty-five when he wrote the following letter to Barry M. Goldwater, sixty-seven:

———

*Goldwater was considered quite conservative when he ran for president, but he became more moderate in later years. For example, he was later critical of Richard Nixon and the Moral Majority.

Honorable Barry Goldwater
United States Senate
Washington, D. C. 20510
Dear Barry:

Monday night at Utah State University, I received a handsome bound volume containing your marvelous letter of March 18, 1976, which Eudora* and I both treasure.

Yes, you are right, as usual. I am not going to sit on the sidelines. I am accepting a research professorship at the University of Utah to do some important projects that I have accumulated over the years. In addition, I was called in April to serve as a Regional Representative of the Council of the Twelve of the Church, with two regions and eight stakes to superintend. Also, July 1 I take office as President of the Salt Lake Rotary Club and will look after those 400 Rotarians in the Hotel Utah weekly, plus a lot of other things.

While writing, let me remark that we always look for your appearances on "Face the Nation," "Meet the Press,"† or other opportunities, and are much appreciative of the sober, sound sense you articulate so well—not to mention the very great service you and John Rhodes‡ combined to render for our country in the resignation of one President [Richard M. Nixon] and the ascent to office of President [Gerald R.] Ford. You have gained an indelible place in the history of the nation and, in so doing, have

---

*Eudora Widtsoe Durham, daughter of Apostle John A. Widtsoe and Leah Dunford Widtsoe. She and G. Homer Durham were married on 20 June 1936.

†Television news programs.

‡Republican Congressman from Arizona who was House minority leader when Richard Nixon resigned in 1974.

made Arizona and what it stands for something to be reckoned with forever after.

Thanks again for a wonderful letter.

Sincerely yours,

G. Homer Durham

Commissioner of Higher Education

And Chief Executive Officer

Elder Durham's letter itself offers good evidence of his high energy and just a few of his accomplishments. During his long career as an educator, he also taught at Utah State University, Swarthmore College, and the University of Utah and was a visiting faculty member at UCLA.

In his first talk after becoming a General Authority, less than a year after writing the above letter, Elder Durham said, "My dear brethren of the priesthood, I would like you to know that with deep humility I accept the call to service as a member of the First Quorum of the Seventy. I pledge to the Lord, to these brethren of the General Authorities, and to you, my life, my labors, and whatever talents I possess. And my dear wife, Eudora, joins me in this covenant. We are grateful for the love and support we feel from you, my brethren, and from our family and loved ones. And I am grateful that her life has been spared as my companion as we embark in this great service."[2]

Endnotes

Part 1: Husbands and Wives

Joseph Smith to Emma Hale Smith, 6 June 1832

Chicago Historical Society, Chicago, Illinois. For additional background, see Hill, 140–49; and Newell and Avery, 44–45. For more information on the letter itself, see Berrett, "An Impressive Letter from the Pen of Joseph Smith," and Jessee, *Personal Writings*, 237–40. The latter includes a photocopy of the original letter. For more information on Sophronia and Calvin Stoddard, see Bushman, 66–68; Smith, *Biographical Sketches*, 96; and Vogel, I, 58. For more information on Julia Murdock Smith, see Newell and Avery, 253–61; 306.

For an exact transcription of the letter see *BYU Studies*, Vol. 11, 1970–71, Number 4, Summer 1971.

Emma Hale Smith to Joseph Smith, 25 April 1837

Joseph Smith letterbook, LDS Church Archives, Joseph Smith Collection, 1827–1844. For more information on the background of the letter, see Newell and Avery, 62–63; Allen and Leonard, 117–25; and Hill, 205–17.

1. Allen and Leonard, 120.

2. Hill, 209.

3. Ibid., 209.

4. Emma Smith to Joseph Smith, 9 March 1839, Joseph Smith letterbook, LDS Church Archives; cited in Newell and Avery, 79.

Phoebe Carter Woodruff to Wilford Woodruff, 18 July 1840

Excerpts from this letter were first published in Cowley, 151. The version printed here has been edited slightly for readability; it has been compiled from various sources, chiefly Cowley and Staker. See Staker, 38–39 for an exact transcription.

1. Cowley, v.

The letter is copied in Wilford Woodruff's journal.

Diantha Farr Clayton to William Clayton, 16 March 1846

Clayton Papers, LDS Church Archives. For background information relating to the letter, see Allen, 198–204.

1. Allen, 69.

2. William Clayton journal, LDS Church Archives; cited in Allen, 203.

Camilla Eyring Kimball to Spencer W. Kimball, 14 November 1933

Spencer W. Kimball to Camilla Eyring Kimball, November 1933
Both letters reprinted from Kimball and Kimball, *Spencer W. Kimball*, 137–43.
1. *Spencer W. Kimball*, 137.
2. Ibid., 143.

Ezra Taft Benson to Flora Amussen Benson, 17 September 1946
Reprinted from *A Labor of Love*, 189–90.
1. Babbel, 148–49; cited in *Church History in the Fulness of Times*, 539.

Hugh B. Brown to Zina Card Brown, 25 December 1962
Reprinted from Campbell and Poll, 239.
1. Campbell and Poll, 39–43.
2. Firmage, 46.

PART 2: BELOVED FAMILIES

Mary Fielding Smith to Joseph Fielding, June 1839
Reprinted from Smith, *Life of Joseph F. Smith*, 143–46.
1. Pratt, 128.
2. Carr, Cannon, and Cowan, 1137.

John Taylor to His Family, 1850
Reprinted from Roberts, 206–9.
1. Roberts, 203.
2. Taylor, 148–49.

Joseph F. Smith to Joseph Fielding Smith, 20 June 1899
Reprinted from Smith and Kenney, *From Prophet to Son*, 62–64.
1. Smith, *The Life of Joseph Fielding Smith*, 91.
2. Ibid., 162.

Charles A. Callis to Kathleen Callis Larsen, 10 December 1927
Charles A. Callis Collection, L. Tom Perry Special Collections Library, Brigham Young University. Exact transcription of original holograph.

John A. Widtsoe and Leah Eudora Dunford Widtsoe to Susa Young Gates, 19 March 1930
Susa Young Gates Collection, Utah State Historical Society. Elder Widtsoe's letter is typed, with a handwritten signature, on stationery with the following letterhead:
CHURCH OF JESUS CHRIST OF LATTER-DAY SAINTS
OFFICE OF THE EUROPEAN MISSION
295 EDGE LANE LIVERPOOL

Elder Widtsoe's letter is edited slightly. Leah's letter (reproduced as is) is a handwritten addition on the second page of Elder Widtsoe's letter.

1. Richard L. Evans, *Improvement Era*, January 1953.

Zina Young Card to Susa Young Gates, 22 January 1931

Susa Young Gates Collection, Utah State Historical Society.

1. John D. Higginbotham, *When the West Was Young*, cited in the *Improvement Era*, July, 1937.

2. R. Paul Cracroft, "Susa Young Gates: Her Life and Literary Work," master's thesis, University of Utah, 1951, 73; cited in *Encyclopedia of Mormonism*, 535.

3. Some sources (such as Leonard Arrington, *Brigham Young*, 420) give the spelling *Prescinda*.

Joseph Fielding Smith to Lewis Smith, 24 January 1934

Reprinted from Smith, *The Life of Joseph Fielding Smith*, 301–304.

1. Smith, 288.

David O. McKay to His Sons and Daughters, 25 October 1934

Reprinted from McKay, *My Father, David O. McKay*, 193–96.

1. McKay, 191.

2. Ibid., 266.

Harold B. Lee to Helen Lee Goates, 21 November 1946

Courtesy of the late Helen Lee Goates and the *Ensign*. Also printed in Goates, *Harold B. Lee*, 200–201.

PART 3: FRIENDS IN ZION

Joseph Smith to Oliver Cowdery, 22 October 1829

Joseph Smith Letterbook, Joseph Smith Papers, LDS Church Archives, Salt Lake City, Utah. For more information on the translation and printing of the Book of Mormon, see Bushman, 79–113 and Backman, 97–130; 169–200.

1. Smith, *Biographical Sketches*, 127–28.

2. John H. Gilbert to James T. Cobb, 10 February 1879, cited in Backman, 181.

Oliver Cowdery to Phineas H. Young, 23 March 1846

Oliver Cowdery Papers, LDS Church Archives, Salt Lake City, Utah. For more information on Oliver Cowdery's decade out of the Church, see Anderson, "Oliver Cowdery, Esq.," and Faulring.

1. Cannon and Cook, *Far West Record*, 162–71.

2. Reuben Miller, "Last Days of Oliver Cowdery," *Deseret News* 9 (13 April 1859). Reprinted in *Millennial Star* 21 (1859): 544–46; cited in Vogel, Vol. 2, 495.

3. Cook, *David Whitmer Interviews*, 33. Joseph F. Smith made this record in his diary after interviewing David Whitmer with Orson Pratt in September of 1878.

George Albert Smith to Reed Smoot, 9 April 1912

Reed Smoot Collection, L. Tom Perry Special Collections Library, Harold B. Lee Library, Brigham Young University. Typescript, with signature and postscript both handwritten. Reproduced as is.

1. Pusey, 203.
2. Ibid., 246.
3. Ibid., 203.
4. Garr, Cannon, and Cowan, 1117.

Susa Young Gates to Amy Brown Lyman, April 1916

Amy Brown Lyman Collection, L. Tom Perry Special Collections Library, Harold B. Lee Library, Brigham Young University. Exact transcription of original holograph.

Julina Lambson Smith to Reed Smoot, 21 March 1920

Reed Smoot to Julina Lambson Smith, 6 April 1920

Reed Smoot Collection, L. Tom Perry Special Collections Library, Harold B. Lee Library, Brigham Young University. Smith letter is exact transcription of original holograph. Smoot letter is unsigned typescript, reproduced as is.

1. Holzapfel and Shupe, 40.
2. Ibid., 229.
3. Merrill, 6.

J. Golden Kimball to Levi Edgar Young, 7 January 1931

Levi Edgar Young Collection, Utah State Historical Society. Exact transcription of original holograph.

1. Parry and Morris, 29.
2. *Improvement Era*, October 1938, 590.
3. Ibid., 636.

Matthew Cowley to the Elkington Family, 20 May 1943

Reprinted from Smith, *Matthew Cowley*, 239–41.

1. *Improvement Era*, January 1954.

Belle S. Spafford to Ethel Taylor Sessions, 1950

Belle S. Spafford Collection, L. Tom Perry Special Collections Library, Brigham Young University. Typescript with handwritten signature on simple stationery that reads "Belle S. Spafford." Reproduced as is.

1. *Ensign*, November 1974.

Hugh B. Brown to Adam S. Bennion, 7 April 1953

Adam S. Bennion Collection, L. Tom Perry Special Collections Library, Harold B. Lee Library, Brigham Young University. Typescript, with signature handwritten; reproduced as is. Typed on stationery for "Hugh B. Brown, Barrister and Solicitor, 9929 103rd Street, Edmonton, Canada, Phone 42275."

1. Firmage, 112.

2. Ibid., 127.

Spencer W. Kimball to Delbert L. Stapley, 4 August 1957

Copy of original typescript, courtesy of Edward L. Kimball. Unsigned; reproduced as is.

1. Kimball and Kimball, *Spencer W. Kimball*, 263.

2. Ibid., 311.

J. Willard Marriott to Gordon B. Hinckley, 29 April 1958

J. Willard Marriott Collection, University of Utah Special Collections. Typescript; reproduced as is.

1. Dew, 194.

2. Ibid., 370.

G. Homer Durham to Thomas S. Monson, 30 June 1976

G. Homer Durham Collection, University of Utah Special Collections. Typescript, with handwritten signature, on stationery for the State Board of Regents, Utah System of Higher Education. Reproduced as is.

1. *Ensign*, May 1992.

PART 4: THE WORK OF THE KINGDOM

Oliver Cowdery to W. W. Phelps, 7 September 1834

Latter Day Saints' Messenger and Advocate 1 (October 1834): 13–16. This was the first of eight letters from Oliver Cowdery to W. W. Phelps that were published in the *Messenger and Advocate*. In addition, excerpts from this letter are published as a footnote in Joseph Smith–History.

1. W. W. Phelps to E. D. Howe, 15 January 1831; cited in Vogel, vol. 3, 6–7.

Brigham Young to Lucy Mack Smith, 4 April 1847

Brigham Young Papers, LDS Church Archives. Handwritten document in the handwriting of Willard Richards. The version printed here is slightly edited.

1. Eliza R. Snow diary, 10 August 1846, in Maureen Ursenbach Beecher, ed., *The Personal Writings of Eliza Roxcy Snow* (Salt Lake City: University of Utah Press, 1995), 139; cited in Madsen, 307.

2. Journal History, 16 April 1847, LDS Church Archives; cited in Garr, Cannon, and Cowan, 1350.

3. Martha Ann Harris, Centennial Jubilee letter, 22 March 1881, to her children. Don Cecil Corbett. *Mary Fielding, Daughter of Britain* (Salt Lake City: Deseret Book, 1966), 195.

4. Journal and reminiscences of Hannah Tapfield King, 12 May 1853, LDS Church Archives; cited in Newell and Avery, 265.

Lorenzo Snow to Franklin D. Richards, 18 February 1852

Reprinted from Smith, *Biography and Family Record of Lorenzo Snow*, 207–10.

1. Smith, 232.

Eliza R. Snow to Aurelia Spencer Rogers, 4 August 1878

Reprinted from Rogers, 209–11.

1. Rogers, 34–35, 41.

2. Ibid., 208.

Heber J. Grant to Amy Brown Lyman, 27 November 1918

Amy Brown Lyman Collection, L. Tom Perry Special Collections, Harold B. Lee Library, Brigham Young University. Reproduced as is. Typescript, with handwritten signature in Heber J. Grant's incomparable hand, on stationery with the following letterhead:

CHURCH OF JESUS CHRIST OF LATTER-DAY SAINTS

OFFICE OF THE COUNCIL OF THE TWELVE

HEBER J. GRANT, PRESIDENT

SALT LAKE CITY, UTAH

1. Jenson, 756.

2. Gibbons, 172–73.

James E. Talmage to Charles A. Callis, 5 September 1931

Charles A. Callis Collection, L. Tom Perry Special Collections, Harold B. Lee Library, Brigham Young University; typescript, with handwritten signature, on Council of the Twelve letterhead. Reproduced as is.

1. Bennett, 49.

2. Charles A. Callis to Mr. and Mrs. S. Larsen, 10 November 1933, Callis Collection, BYU.

3. George Albert Smith to Mrs. Grace E. Callis, 10 October 1933, Callis Collection, BYU.

4. Charles A. Callis to Kathleen Larsen, 20 January 1947, Callis Collection, BYU.

Nigerian Investigators to the Missionary Department, 13 March 1972

Obinna Brothers to the First Presidency, 1 December 1978

Cannon Papers, LDS Church Archives. Both letters are typescript, with handwritten signatures. Both reproduced as they are. For both letters, copyright is retained by authors.

1. LeBaron, "Steadfast African Pioneer," 45–46.

2. Glen C. Fisher to S. C. Brewerton, M.D.; cited in Morrison, 84.

3. Obinna, 30.

4. *New Era*, April 1980, 36.

5. Morrison, 144.

Gordon B. Hinckley to J. Willard Marriott, 17 April 1985

J. Willard Marriott Collection, University of Utah Special Collections. Typescript, with handwritten signature; reproduced as is. Typed on the following letterhead:

THE CHURCH OF JESUS CHRIST OF LATTER-DAY SAINTS

47 EAST SOUTH TEMPLE STREET

SALT LAKE CITY, UTAH 84111

GORDON B. HINCKLEY

1. *Ensign*, May 1985, 1.
2. Monson, 34.
3. McConkie, 11.
4. *Church News*, 25 August 1985, 10.

Vance Taylor to Howard W. Hunter, 16 January 1992

Courtesy of Vance Taylor and the Howard W. Hunter family. Special thanks to Louine B. Hunter.
1. *Church News*, 11 March 1995.
2. Arrington, *Adventures*, 84.
3. Todd, 4–5.
4. Huntsman, 25.

Jon M. Huntsman to an Individual Seeking Counsel, circa 1995

Courtesy of Jon M. Huntsman.
1. Nelson, 16.
2. *Church News*, 25 October 1997.

PART 5: FELLOWSHIP WITH PUBLIC FIGURES

Joseph Smith to John Wentworth, 1 March 1842

Times and Seasons (Nauvoo, Illinois), 3 (1 March 1842): 706–10.
1. Roberts, *A Comprehensive History*, 1:55n.

Reed Smoot to Theodore Roosevelt, 27 May 1904

Theodore Roosevelt to Reed Smoot, 2 June 1904

Reed Smoot Collection, L. Tom Perry Special Collections, Harold B. Lee Library, Brigham Young University. Smoot letter is an unsigned typescript, reproduced as is (including misspelling of Roosevelt's first name). Roosevelt letter is a signed typescript, reproduced as is, on stationery with the following letterhead:
WHITE HOUSE,
WASHINGTON.
1. Merrill, 28.
2. Garr, Cannon, and Cowan, 1146.
3. Merrill, 41.
4. Firmage, 31–32.

Herbert Hoover to J. Reuben Clark Jr. 13 November 1941

J. Reuben Clark Jr. Collection, L. Tom Perry Special Collections, Harold B. Lee Library, Brigham Young University. Typescript, with handwritten signature, reproduced as is. Letterhead reads "HERBERT HOOVER."
1. J. Reuben Clark Jr. Collection, BYU.
2. Quinn, 213.

J. Edgar Hoover to J. Willard Marriott, 7 May 1958

> J. Willard Marriott Collection, J. Willard Marriott Library, University of Utah. Typescript, with hand-written signature, reproduced as is. The stationery has the following letterhead:
> UNITED STATES DEPARTMENT OF JUSTICE
> FEDERAL BUREAU OF INVESTIGATION

G. Homer Durham to Barry Goldwater, 28 May 1976

> G. Homer Durham Collection, Special Collections, J. Willard Marriott Library, University of Utah. Unsigned, corrected typescript; reproduced as corrected.
>
> 1. Goldwater, xiii.
>
> 2. Durham, 41.

BIOGRAPHICAL SUMMARIES

Adam S. Bennion. Born 2 December 1886 in Taylorsville, Utah, to Joseph Bennion and Mary Sharp. Married Minerva Young 14 September 1911. Five children. Ordained an apostle 9 April 1953 at age sixty-six by David O. McKay. Died 11 February 1958 at age seventy-one.

Ezra Taft Benson. Born 4 August 1899 in Whitney, Idaho, to George Taft Benson and Sarah Dunkley. Married Flora Smith Amussen 10 September 1926. Six children. Ordained an apostle 7 October 1943 at age forty-four by Heber J. Grant. (Ordained the same day but directly after Spencer W. Kimball.) Ordained President of the Church 10 November 1985 at age eighty-six. Died 30 May 1994 in Salt Lake City at age ninety-four. For more information, see Babbel, *On Wings of Faith*; Benson, *A Labor of Love*; and Sheri L. Dew, *Ezra Taft Benson: A Biography* (Salt Lake City: Deseret Book, 1987).

Flora Smith Amussen Benson. Born 1 July 1901 in Logan, Utah, to Carl Amussen and Barbara Smith. Married Ezra Taft Benson 10 September 1926. Six children. Died 14 August 1992 in Salt Lake City at age ninety-one. For more information, see Derin Head Rodriguez, "Flora Amussen Benson: Handmaiden of the Lord, Helpmeet of a Prophet, Mother in Zion," *Ensign*, March 1987, 15–20.

Hugh B. Brown. Born 24 October 1883 in Granger, Utah, to Homer Manley Brown and Lydia Jane Brown. Married Zina Young Card 17 June 1908. Eight children. Sustained as an Assistant to the Twelve 4 October 1953 at age sixty-nine. Ordained an apostle 10 April 1958 at age seventy-four by David O. McKay. Died 2 December 1975 in Salt Lake City at age ninety-two.

For more information, see Firmage, *An Abundant Life: The Memoirs of Hugh B. Brown*, and Campbell and Poll, *Hugh B. Brown: His Life and Thought*.

Zina Young Card Brown. Born 12 June 1888 in Cardston, Alberta, Canada, to Charles Ora Card and Zina Presendia Young. Married Hugh B. Brown 17 June 1908. Eight children. Died 19 December 1974 in Salt Lake City at age eighty-six.

Charles A. Callis. Born 4 May 1865 in Dublin, Ireland, to John Callis and Susannah Charlotte Quillam. Married Grace Elizabeth Pack 3 September 1902. (She died 15 October 1946.) Ordained an apostle 11 October 1933 at age sixty-eight by Heber J. Grant. Died 21 January 1947 in Jacksonville, Florida, at age eighty-one.

Zina Presendia Young Card. Born 3 April 1850 in Salt Lake City to Brigham Young and Zina D. Huntington. Married Thomas Williams 12 October 1868. (He died 17 July 1874.) Two children. Married Charles Ora Card 17 June 1884. (He died 9 September 1906.) Three children. Died 31 January 1931 in Salt Lake City at age eighty.

J. Reuben Clark Jr. Born 1 September 1871 in Grantsville, Utah, to Joshua Reuben Clark and Mary Woolley. Married Luacine Savage 14 September 1898. (She died 2 August 1944.) Sustained as second counselor to Heber J. Grant 6 April 1933 at age sixty-one. Ordained an apostle 11 October 1934 at age sixty-three by Heber J. Grant. Counselor to three Church presidents—Heber J. Grant, George Albert Smith, and David O. McKay—serving in the First Presidency until his death on 6 October 1961 in Salt Lake City at age ninety. For more information, see Frank Fox, *J. Reuben Clark: The Public Years* (Provo, Utah: Brigham Young University Press, 1980); and Quinn, *J. Reuben Clark: The Church Years*.

Diantha Farr Clayton. Born 12 October 1828 in Charleston, Vermont, to Winslow Farr and Olive Freeman. Married William Clayton 9 January 1845 in Nauvoo. Three children—Moroni (31 March 1846–4 October 1864), Olive

Diantha (7 August 1848–13 October 1915), and Rachel Amelia (18 August 1850–4 April 1872). Died 11 September 1850 in Salt Lake City at age twenty-one.

William Clayton. Born 17 July 1814 in Penwortham, England, to Thomas Clayton and Ann Critchely. Married Ruth Moon in 1836. (She died in 1894.) Took nine additional wives between 1843 and 1870. Died 4 December 1879 in Salt Lake City at age sixty-five. For more information see Allen, *Trials of Discipleship: The Story of William Clayton, a Mormon.*

Oliver Cowdery. Born 3 October 1806 in Wells, Vermont, to William Cowdery Jr., and Rebecca Fuller. Ordained an apostle with Joseph Smith by Peter, James, and John sometime in the spring of 1829 (the date is not certain). Charter member of the Church, 6 April 1830. Married Elizabeth Ann Whitmer 18 December 1832. (She died 7 January 1892.) Six children, five of whom died in infancy; no grandchildren. Ordained Assistant President of the Church 5 December 1834. Excommunicated 12 April 1838 in Far West, Missouri. Rebaptized by Orson Hyde 12 November 1848 at Council Bluffs, Iowa. Died 3 March 1850 in Richmond, Missouri, at age forty-three. For more information see Anderson; Faulring; Gunn; Morris; and Vogel, vol. 2.

Matthew Cowley. Born 2 August 1897 in Preston, Idaho, to Matthias F. Cowley and Abigail Hyde. Married Elva Taylor 18 July 1922. (She died 18 August 1987.) Ordained an apostle 11 October 1945 at age forty-eight by George Albert Smith. Died 13 December 1953 in Los Angeles, California, at age fifty-six.

G. Homer Durham. Born 4 February 1911 in Parowan, Utah, to George Durham and Mary Ellen Marsden. Married Leah Eudora Widtsoe 20 June 1936. Sustained to the First Quorum of the Seventy 2 April 1977 at age sixty-six. Died 10 January 1985 in Salt Lake City at age seventy-three.

Joseph Fielding. Born 26 March 1797 in Honeydon, Bedfordshire, England, to John Fielding and Rachel Ibbotson. Married Hannah Greenwood 11 June

1838. (She died 9 September 1877). Seven children. Took two additional wives in Nauvoo. Died 19 December 1863 in Mill Creek, Utah, at age sixty-six.

Susa Young Gates. Born 18 March 1856 in Salt Lake City to Brigham Young and Lucy Bigelow. Married Alma Dunford 1 December 1872; later divorced. (He died 1 February 1919.) Two children. Married Jacob Gates 5 January 1880. (He died 22 January 1942.) Eleven children. Died 27 May 1933 in Salt Lake City at age seventy-seven.

Helen Lee Goates. Born 25 November 1925 in Salt Lake City to Harold B. Lee and Fern Lucinda Tanner. Married L. Brent Goates 24 June 1946. Died 19 April 2000 in Salt Lake City at age seventy-four.

Barry Goldwater. Born 1 January 1909 in Phoenix, Arizona, to Baron Goldwater and Josephine Williams. Married Peggy Johnson 22 September 1934. (She died 11 December 1985.) Served in the U.S. Senate from 1953–64 and 1969–86. Died 29 May 1998 at age eighty-nine.

Heber J. Grant. Born 22 November 1856 in Salt Lake City to Jedediah M. Grant and Rachel Ivins. Married Lucy Stingham 1 November 1877. (She died 3 January 1893.) Six children. Married Hulda Augusta Winters 26 May 1884. One child. Married Emily Wells 27 May 1884. (She died 25 May 1908.) Five children. Ordained an apostle 16 October 1882 at age twenty-five by George Q. Cannon. Ordained President of the Church 23 November 1918 at age sixty-two. Died 14 May 1945 in Salt Lake City at age eighty-eight.

Hulda Augusta ("Gusta") Winters Grant. Born 7 July 1856 in Payson, Utah, to Oscar Winters and Mary Ann Stearns. Married Heber J. Grant 26 May 1884. One child. Died 1 June 1952 in Salt Lake City at age ninety-five.

Gordon B. Hinckley. Born 23 June 1910 in Salt Lake City to Bryant S. Hinckley and Ada Bitner. Married Marjorie Pay 29 April 1937. Sustained an Assistant to the Twelve 6 April 1958. Ordained an apostle 5 October 1961 at age fifty-one by David O. McKay. Ordained President of the Church 12 March 1995 at age eighty-four.

Herbert Hoover. Born 10 August 1874 in West Branch, Iowa, to Jesse Clark Hoover and Hulda Randall Minthorn. Married Lou Henry 10 February 1899. (She died 7 January 1944.) Two children. Served as United States President from 1929–33. Died 20 October 1964 in New York City at age ninety.

J. Edgar Hoover. Born 1 January 1895. Never married. Died 2 May 1972 at age seventy-seven. Served as director of the FBI from 1924 until his death.

Jon M. Huntsman. Born 21 June 1937 in Blackfoot, Idaho. Married Karen Haight. Nine children.

Howard W. Hunter. Born 14 November 1907 in Boise, Idaho, to John William Hunter and Nellie Marie Rasmussen. Married Clara May (Claire) Jeffs 10 June 1931. (She died 9 October 1983.) Three children. Married Inis Bernice Egan 12 April 1990. Ordained an apostle 15 October 1959 at age fifty-one by David O. McKay. Ordained President of the Church 5 June 1994 at age eighty-six. Died 3 March 1995 in Salt Lake City at age eighty-seven.

Camilla Eyring Kimball. Born 7 December 1894 in Colonia Juarez, Mexico, to Edward Eyring and Caroline Cottam Romney. Married Spencer W. Kimball 16 November 1917. Four children. Died 20 September 1987 in Salt Lake City at age ninety-two. For more information, see Edward L. Kimball and Caroline Eyring Miner, *Camilla: A Biography of Camilla Eyring Kimball* (Salt Lake City: Deseret Book, 1980).

J. Golden Kimball. Born 9 June 1853 in Salt Lake City to Heber C. Kimball and Christeen Golden. Married Jane ("Jennie") Knowlton 22 September 1887. (She died 25 August 1940.) Sustained as one of the First Seven Presidents of the Seventy 5 April 1892 at age thirty-eight; set apart by

Francis M. Lyman. Died in an automobile accident 2 September 1938 near Reno, Nevada, at age eighty-five.

Spencer W. Kimball. Born 28 March 1895 in Salt Lake City to Andrew Kimball and Olive Wooley. Married Camilla Eyring 16 November 1917. Four children. Ordained an apostle 7 October 1943 at age forty-eight by Heber J. Grant. Ordained President of the Church 30 December 1973 at age seventy-eight. Died 5 November 1985 in Salt Lake City at age ninety. For specific information on President Kimball's time in the hospital, see his book One Silent Sleepless Night (Salt Lake City: Bookcraft, 1975). For general information on President Kimball, see Edward L. Kimball and Andrew E. Kimball, Jr., Spencer W. Kimball, as well as the complete issue of BYU Studies 25 (Fall 1985).

Kathleen Callis Larsen. Born circa 1905 to Charles A. Callis and Grace Pack. Married Spencer Larsen. (He died 28 May 1979.)

Harold B. Lee. Born 28 March 1899 in Clifton, Idaho, to Samuel Lee and Louisa Bingham. Married Fern Lucinda Tanner 14 November 1923. (She died 24 September 1962.) Two children. Married Freda Joan Jensen 17 June 1963. Ordained an apostle 10 April 1941 at age forty-two by Heber J. Grant. Ordained President of the Church 7 July 1972 at age seventy-three. Died 26 December 1973 in Salt Lake City at age seventy-four. For more information, see L. Brent Goates, Harold B. Lee, and Goates, He Changed My Life: Personal Experiences with Harold B. Lee (Salt Lake City: Bookcraft, 1988).

Amy Brown Lyman. Born 7 February 1872 in Pleasant Grove, Utah, to John Brown and Margaret Zimmerman. Married Richard R. Lyman 9 September 1896. (He died 31 December 1963.) Two children: Wendell (1897–1933) and Margaret (1903–1985). First Counselor to Louise Y. Robison in General Relief Society Presidency from October 1928 to December 1939. General president of the Relief Society from 1 January 1940 to 6 April 1945. Died 5 December 1959 in Salt Lake City at age eighty-seven.

David O. McKay. Born 8 September 1873 in Huntsville, Utah, to David McKay and Jenette Evans. Married Emma Ray Riggs 2 January 1901. (She died 14 November 1970.) Ordained an apostle 9 April 1906 at age thirty-two by Joseph F. Smith. Sustained as President of the Church 9 April 1951 at age seventy-seven. Died 18 January 1970 in Salt Lake City at age ninety-six. For more information, see David Lawrence McKay, My *Father, David O. McKay*; Llewelyn McKay, comp., *Home Memories of President David O. McKay* (Salt Lake City: Deseret Book, 1956); Clare Middlemiss, comp., *Man May Know for Himself*; and Jeannette McKay Morrell, *Highlights in the Life of President David O. McKay* (Salt Lake City: Deseret Book, 1966).

J. Willard Marriott. Born 17 September 1900 in Marriott, Utah, to Hyrum Willard and Ellen Morris. Married Alice Sheets 9 June 1927. (She died 18 April 2000.) Two children. Died 13 August 1985 at age eighty-four.

Thomas S. Monson. Born 21 August 1927 in Salt Lake City to G. Spencer Monson and Gladys Condie. Married Frances Beverly Johnson 7 October 1948. Three children. Ordained an apostle 10 October 1963 at age thirty-six by David O. McKay. Set apart as member of the First Presidency 10 November 1985.

Anthony Obinna. Born 15 April 1928 in Aboh Mbaisi, Nigeria. First black branch president in Africa. Wife Fidelia was first black Relief Society president in Africa. Died 25 August 1995 in Aboh Mbaisi at age sixty-seven.

William Wines (W. W.) Phelps. Born 17 February 1792 in Hanover, New Jersey, to Enon Phelps and Mehitable Goldsmith. Married Sally Waterman 28 April 1815. Excommunicated 1838; reinstated to fellowship 1840. Excommunicated and rebaptized in December of 1847. Died 6 March 1872 in Salt Lake City at age eighty. For more information, see Cook, *The Revelations of the Prophet Joseph Smith*, 87–88.

Franklin D. Richards. Born 2 April 1821 in Richmond, Massachusetts, to Phinehas Richards and Wealthy Dewey. Ordained an apostle 12 February

1849 at age twenty-seven by Heber C. Kimball. Died 9 December 1899 in Ogden, Utah, at age seventy-eight.

Aurelia Spencer Rogers. Born 4 October 1834 in Deep River, Connecticut, to Orson Spencer and Catherine Curtis. Married Thomas Rogers 27 March 1851. (He died 18 September 1896.) Twelve children. First ward Primary president, 1878 (Farmington Ward, Davis Utah Stake). Died 19 August 1922 in Farmington, Utah, at age eighty-seven.

Theodore Roosevelt. Born 27 October 1858 in New York City. Married Alice Lee in 1880. (She died in 1884). One child. Married Edith Carow in 1886. (She died in 1948.) Five children. United States president from 1901 to 1909. Died 6 January 1919 in Sagamore Hill, Oyster Bay, New York, at age sixty.

Ethel Taylor Sessions. Born 26 April 1892 in Provo, Utah, to Thomas Taylor and Maud Rogers. Married Harvey Sessions 29 September 1936.

Emma Hale Smith (Bidamon). Born 10 July 1804 in Harmony, Pennsylvania, to Isaac Hale and Elizabeth Lewis. Married Joseph Smith Jr. 18 January 1827. Nine children: Alvin (born and died 15 June 1828); Thaddeus (born and died 30 April 1831); Louisa (born and died 30 April 1831); Joseph (6 November 1832–10 December 1914); Frederick Granger Williams (20 June 1836–13 April 1862); Alexander Hale (2 June 1838–12 August 1909); Don Carlos (13 June 1840–15 September 1841); unnamed son (born and died 6 February 1842); David Hyrum (18 November 1844–29 August 1904). Served as first general president of the Relief Society from 17 March 1842 to 16 March 1844. Married Lewis C. Bidamon 23 December 1847. No children. Died 30 April 1879 in Nauvoo, Illinois, at age seventy-four. For more information on Emma Hale Smith, see Newell and Avery. Important interviews given by Emma Hale Smith are included in Vogel, vol. 1.

George Albert Smith. Born 4 April 1870 in Salt Lake City to John Henry Smith and Sarah Farr. Married Lucy Woodruff 25 May 1892. (She died

5 November 1937.) Three children. Ordained an apostle 8 October 1903 at age thirty-three by Joseph F. Smith. Ordained President of the Church 21 May 1945 at age seventy-five. Died 4 April 1951, on his eighty-first birthday, in Salt Lake City.

Joseph Smith Jr. Born 23 December 1805 in Sharon, Vermont, to Joseph Smith Sr. and Lucy Mack. Married Emma Hale 18 January 1827. Nine children. Ordained an apostle with Oliver Cowdery by Peter, James, and John in the spring of 1829 (the date is not certain). Sustained as First Elder of the Church 6 April 1830 at age twenty-four. Sustained as president of the High Priesthood 25 January 1832 at age twenty-six. Martyred 27 June 1844 at Carthage Jail, Illinois, at age thirty-eight. For more information on Joseph Smith see Bushman, Hill, all three volumes of Jesse, and all three volumes of Vogel.

Joseph F. Smith. Born 13 November 1838 in Far West, Missouri, to Hyrum Smith and Mary Fielding. Married Levira Smith 4 April 1859. (She died 18 December 1888.) Later divorced; no children. Married Julina Lambson 5 May 1866. Thirteen children. Married Sarah Ellen Richards 1 March 1868. (She died 22 March 1915.) Eleven children. Married Edna Lambson 1 January 1871. (She died 28 February 1926.) Ten children. Married Alice Ann Kimball 6 December 1883. (She died 19 December 1946.) Seven children. Married Mary Taylor Schwartz 13 January 1884. (She died 5 December 1956.) Seven children. Ordained an apostle 1 July 1866 at age twenty-seven by Brigham Young. Ordained President of the Church 17 October 1901 at age sixty-two. Died 19 November 1918 in Salt Lake City at age eighty. For more information, see Holzapfel; and Joseph Fielding Smith, *Life of Joseph F. Smith* (Salt Lake City: Deseret Book, 1938).

Joseph Fielding Smith. Born 19 July 1876 in Salt Lake City to Joseph F. Smith and Julina Lambson. Married Louie E. Shurtliff 26 April 1898. (She died 30 March 1908). Two children. Married Ethel G. Reynolds 2 November 1908. (She died 26 August 1937.) Nine children. Married Jesse Ella Evans

12 April 1938. (She died 3 August 1971.) Ordained an apostle 7 April 1910 at age thirty-three by his father Joseph F. Smith. Ordained President of the Church 23 January 1970 at age ninety-three. Died 2 July 1972 in Salt Lake City at age ninety-five. For more information on Joseph Fielding Smith, see Smith, *The Life of Joseph Fielding Smith,* and Joseph F. McConkie, *True and Faithful: The Life Story of Joseph Fielding Smith* (Salt Lake City: Bookcraft, 1971).

Julina Lambson Smith. Born 18 June 1849 in Salt Lake City to Alfred Lambson and Melissa Jane Bigler. Married Joseph F. Smith 5 May 1866. Thirteen children. Served as second counselor to Emmeline B. Wells in the Relief Society general presidency 3 October 1910 to 2 April 1921. Died 10 January 1936 in Salt Lake City at age eighty-six.

Lewis Warren Smith. Born 10 March 1918 in Salt Lake City to Joseph Fielding Smith and Ethel Georgina Reynolds. Died 29 December 1944 at age twenty-six.

Lucy Mack Smith. Born 8 July 1775 in Gilsum, New Hampshire, to Solomon Mack and Lydia Gates. (Lucy gives 1776 as the year of her birth, but according to the town record, she was born in 1775.) Married Joseph Smith 24 January 1796. Ten children: Alvin (11 February 1799–19 November 1823); Hyrum (9 February 1800–27 June 1844); Sophronia (18 May 1803–1876); Joseph Jr. (23 December 1805–27 June 1844); Samuel Harrison (13 March 1808–30 July 1844); Ephraim (13 March 1810–24 March 1810); William (13 March 1811–13 November 1893); Catherine (8 July 1812–1 February 1900); Don Carlos (25 March 1816–7 August 1841); Lucy (18 July 1821–9 December 1882). Died 14 May 1856 in Nauvoo, Illinois, at age eighty.

Mary Fielding Smith. Born 21 July 1801 in Honeydon, Bedfordshire, England, to John Fielding and Rachel Ibbotson. Married Hyrum Smith 24 December 1837. (He died 27 June 1844.) Two children: Joseph F. and Martha Ann. Died 21 September 1852 in Salt Lake City at age fifty-one.

Reed Smoot. Born 10 January 1862 in Salt Lake City to Abraham Smoot and Anne Morrison. Married Alpha May Eldredge 17 September 1884. (She died 11 November 1928.) Six children. Married Alice Sheets. Ordained an apostle 8 April 1900 at age thirty-eight by Lorenzo Snow. Elected to United States Senate in 1903; served until 1932. Died 9 February 1941 in St. Petersburg, Florida, at age seventy-nine.

Eliza R. Snow. Born 21 January 1804 in Becket, Massachusetts, to Oliver Snow and Rosetta Pettibone. Married Joseph Smith in 1842; no children. Married Brigham Young in 1844; no children. General president of the Relief Society from 1866 to 1887. Died 5 December 1887 in Salt Lake City at age eighty-three.

Lorenzo Snow. Born 3 April 1814 in Mantua, Ohio, to Oliver Snow and Rosetta Pettibone. Nine wives. Forty-two children. Ordained an apostle 12 February 1849 at age thirty-four by Heber C. Kimball. Ordained President of the Church 13 September 1898 at age eighty-four. Died 10 October 1901 in Salt Lake City at age eighty-seven.

Marion Isabell ("Belle") S. Spafford. Born 8 October 1895 in Salt Lake City to John Smith and Hester Sims. Married Willis Earl Spafford 21 March 1921. (He died 26 January 1963.) Two children. General president of the Relief Society from 6 April 1945 to 3 October 1974. Died 2 February 1982 in Salt Lake City at age eighty-six.

Delbert L. Stapley. Born 11 December 1896 in Mesa, Arizona, to Orley S. Stapley and Polly M. Hunsaker. Married Ethel Burdette Davis 14 January 1918. Three children. Ordained an apostle 5 October 1950 at age fifty-three by George Albert Smith. Died 19 August 1978 in Salt Lake City at age eighty-one.

James E. Talmage. Born 21 September 1862 in Hungerford, Berks, England, to Gabriel James Joyce Talmage and Susanna Preater. Married Merry May Booth 14 June 1888. (She died 6 April 1944.) Eight children. Ordained an apostle 8 December 1911 at age forty-nine by Joseph F. Smith. Died 27 July 1933 in Salt Lake City at age seventy.

John Taylor. Born 1 November 1808 in Milnthorpe, England, to James Taylor and Agnes Taylor. Married Leonora Cannon 28 January 1833 in Toronto. Nine wives. Thirty-four children. Ordained an apostle 19 December 1838. Ordained President of the Church 10 October 1880—three years after the death of Brigahm Young. Died 25 July 1887 in Kaysville, Utah, at age seventy-eight. See Roberts and Taylor for more information.

John Wentworth. Born in Sandwich, New York, 1815. Served in U.S. House of Representatives and as mayor of Chicago. Died in 1888 in Chicago, Illinois, at about age seventy-three. For more information see Vogel, vol. 1, 169.

John A. Widtsoe. Born 31 January 1872 in Daloe, Norway, to John Anderson Widtsoe and Anne Karine Pedersen. Married Leah Eudora Dunford 1 June 1898. Seven children. Ordained an apostle 17 March 1921 at age forty-nine by Heber J. Grant. Died 29 November 1952 in Salt Lake City at age eighty.

Leah Eudora Dunford Widtsoe. Born 24 February 1874 in Salt Lake City to Alma Dunford and Susa Young Gates. Married John A. Widtsoe 1 June 1898. Seven children. Died 7 June 1965 in Salt Lake City at age ninety-one.

Phoebe Carter Woodruff. Born 8 March 1807 in Scarboro, Maine, to Ezra Carter and Sarah Fabyan. Married Willford Woodruff 13 April 1837 in Kirtland, Ohio. Nine children—Sarah Emma (14 July 1838–17 July 1840), Wilford (22 March 1840–6 May 1921), Phoebe Amelia (4 March 1842–15 February 1919), Susan Cornelia (25 July 1843–6 October 1897), Joseph Carter (18 July 1845–12 November 1846), Ezra Carter (8 December 1846–10 December 1846), Sarah Carter (28 October 1847–22 July 1848), Beulah Augusta (19 July 1851–13 January 1905), Aphek (born and died 25 January 1853). Died 10 November 1885 in Salt Lake City at age seventy-eight.

Wilford Woodruff. Born 1 March 1807 in Farmington, Connecticut, to Aphek Woodruff and Beulah Thompson. Seven wives. Thirty-three children. Ordained an apostle 26 April 1839 at age thirty-two by Brigham Young. Sustained as President of the Church 7 April 1889. Died 2 September 1898 in San Francisco, California, at age ninety-two. For more information see Cowley and Staker.

Brigham Young. Born 1 June 1801 in Whittingham, Vermont, to John Young and Abigail Howe. Twenty-five wives. Fifty-seven children. Ordained an apostle 14 February 1835 at age thirty-three by Oliver Cowdery, David Whitmer, and Martin Harris. Appointed president of Twelve Apostles 19 January 1841. Ordained President of the Church 5 December 1847 in Kanesville, Iowa, at age forty-five. Died in Salt Lake City 29 August 1877 at age seventy-six. For more information see Arrington, *Brigham Young.*

Levi Edgar Young. Born 2 February 1874 in Salt Lake City to Seymour Young and Ann Riter. Married Valeria Brinton 12 June 1907. Three children. Set apart to the First Council of the Seventy 23 January 1910 at age thirty-five by John Henry Smith. Died 13 December 1963 in Salt Lake City at age eighty-nine.

Phineas H. Young. Born 16 February 1799 in Hopkinton, Massachusetts, to John Young and Abigail Howe. Married Lucy Pearce Cowdery 28 September 1834. Four children. Died 10 October 1879 in Salt Lake City at age eighty.

BIBLIOGRAPHY

ARTICLES

Benson, Ezra Taft. "Beware of Pride." *Ensign*, May 1989, 4–7.

Bennett, Richard E. "Elder Charles A. Callis: Twentieth-Century Missionary." *Ensign*, April 1981, 46–51.

Berrett, Lamar C. "An Impressive Letter from the Pen of Joseph Smith." *BYU Studies* 11 (Summer 1971): 517–23.

Durham, G. Homer. "The Validity of the Gospel." *Ensign*, May 1977, 41–42.

Faulring, Scott H. "The Return of Oliver Cowdery." In Stephen D. Ricks, Donald W. Parry, and Andrew H. Hedges, *The Disciple as Witness: Essays on Latter-day Saint History and Doctrine in Honor of Richard Lloyd Anderson*, 117–73. Provo, Utah: The Foundation for Ancient Research and Mormon Studies at Brigham Young University, 2000.

Hall, David. "Anxiously Engaged: Amy Brown Lyman and Relief Society Charity Work, 1917–45." *Dialogue* 27.2 (Summer 1994): 73–91.

Huntsman, Jon M. "A Remarkable and Selfless Life." *Ensign*, April 1995, 24–25.

LeBaron, E. Dale. "Gospel Pioneers in Africa." *Ensign*, August 1990, 40–43.

———. "Steadfast African Pioneer." *Ensign*, December 1999, 45–49.

McConkie, Bruce R. "The Purifying Power of Gethsemane." *Ensign*, May 1985, 9–11.

Monson, Thomas S. "Our Brothers' Keepers." *Ensign*, June 1998, 33–39.

Morris, Larry E. "Oliver Cowdery's Vermont Years and the Origins of Mormonism." *BYU Studies* 39.1 (2000): 106–29.

Nelson, Russell M. "Drama on the European Stage." *Ensign*, December 1991, 7–17.

Obinna, Anthony Uzodimma. "Voice from Nigeria." *Ensign*, December 1980, 30.

Skousen, Royal. "John Gilbert's 1892 Account of the 1830 Printing of the Book of Mormon." In Stephen D. Ricks, Donald W. Parry, and Andrew H. Hedges, *The Disciple as Witness: Essays on Latter-day Saint History and Doctrine in Honor of Richard Lloyd Anderson*, 383–405. Provo, Utah: The Foundation for Ancient Research and Mormon Studies at Brigham Young University, 2000.

Todd, Jay M. "President Howard W. Hunter: Fourteenth President of the Church." *Ensign*, July 1994, 4–5.

BOOKS

Allen, James B. *Trials of Discipleship: The Story of William Clayton, a Mormon*. Urbana and Chicago: University of Illinois Press, 1987.

Allen, James B., and Glen M. Leonard. *The Story of the Latter-day Saints*. Salt Lake City: Deseret Book, 1976, 1992.

Anderson, Richard Lloyd. *Investigating the Book of Mormon Witnesses*. Salt Lake City: Deseret Book, 1981.

Arrington, Leonard J. *Adventures of a Church Historian*. Urbana and Chicago: University of Illinois Press, 1998.

———. *Brigham Young: American Moses*. Urbana and Chicago: University of Illinois Press, 1986.

Babbel, Frederick W. *On Wings of Faith*. Salt Lake City: Bookcraft, 1972.

Backman, Milton V., Jr. *Eyewitness Accounts of the Restoration*. Salt Lake City: Deseret Book, 1983, 1986.

Benson, Ezra Taft. *A Labor of Love: The 1946 European Mission of Ezra Taft Benson.* Salt Lake City: Deseret Book, 1989.

Bushman, Richard L. *Joseph Smith and the Beginnings of Mormonism.* Urbana and Chicago: University of Illinois Press, 1984.

Campbell, Eugene E., and Richard D. Poll. *Hugh B. Brown: His Life and Thought.* Salt Lake City: Bookcraft, 1975.

Cannon, Donald Q., and Lyndon W. Cook. *Far West Record.* Salt Lake City: Deseret Book, 1983.

Church History in the Fulness of Times: The History of The Church of Jesus Christ of Latter-day Saints. Prepared by the Church Educational System for Religion Courses 341–43. Salt Lake City: The Church of Jesus Christ of Latter-day Saints, 1989.

Cook, Lyndon W. *David Whitmer Interviews: A Restoration Witness.* Orem, Utah: Grandin Book Company, 1991, 1993.

———. *The Revelations of the Prophet Joseph Smith: A Historical and Biographical Commentary on the Doctrine and Covenants.* Salt Lake City: Deseret Book, 1985.

Cowley, Matthias F. *Wilford Woodruff: History of His Life and Labors.* Salt Lake City: Deseret Book, 1901.

Derr, Jill Mulvay, Janath Russell Cannon, and Maureen Ursenbach Beecher. *Women of Covenant: The Story of Relief Society.* Salt Lake City: Deseret Book, 1992.

Deseret News 1999–2000 Church Almanac. Salt Lake City: The Church of Jesus Christ of Latter-day Saints, 1998.

Dew, Sheri L. *Go Forward with Faith: The Biography of Gordon B. Hinckley.* Salt Lake City: Deseret Book, 1996.

Firmage, Edwin B., ed. *An Abundant Life: The Memoirs of Hugh B. Brown.* 2d ed., enlarged. Salt Lake City: Signature Books, 1999.

Funk and Wagnalls New Encyclopedia, 1971–1983.

Garr, Arnold, Donald Q. Cannon, and Richard O. Cowan. *Encyclopedia of Latter-day Saint History*. Salt Lake City: Deseret Book, 2000.

Gibbons, Francis M. *Dynamic Disciples, Prophets of God*. Salt Lake City: Deseret Book, 1996.

Goates, L. Brent. *Harold B. Lee: Prophet and Seer*. Salt Lake City: Bookcraft, 1985.

Goldwater, Barry M., with Jack Casserly. *Goldwater*. New York: Doubleday, 1988.

Gunn, Stanley R. *Oliver Cowdery: Second Elder and Scribe*. Salt Lake City: Bookcraft, 1962.

Hill, Donna. *Joseph Smith: The First Mormon*. Midvale, Utah: Signature Books, 1977.

Holzapfel, Richard Neitzel, and R. Q. Shupe. *Joseph F. Smith: Portrait of a Prophet*. Salt Lake City: Deseret Book, 2000.

Iverson, Peter. *Barry Goldwater: Native Arizonan*. Norman and London: University of Oklahoma Press, 1997.

Jenson, Andrew. *Latter-day Saint Biographical Encyclopedia: A Compilation of Biographical Sketches of Prominent Men and Women in The Church of Jesus Christ of Latter-day Saints*. 4 vols. Salt Lake City: A. Jenson History Company and Deseret News, 1901–1936.

Jesse, Dean C., ed. *The Papers of Joseph Smith, Volume I: Autobiographical and Historical Writings*. Salt Lake City: Deseret Book, 1989.

———. *The Papers of Joseph Smith, Volume II: Journal, 1832–1842*. Salt Lake City: Deseret Book, 1992.

Jesse, Dean C., ed. and comp. *The Personal Writings of Joseph Smith*. Salt Lake City: Deseret Book, 1984.

Kimball, Edward L., and Andrew E. Kimball Jr. *Spencer W. Kimball: Twelfth President of the The Church of Jesus Christ of Latter-day Saints*. Salt Lake City: Bookcraft, 1977.

McKay, Llewelyn, comp. *Home Memories of President David O. McKay*. Salt Lake City: Deseret Book, 1956.

Madsen, Carol Cornwall. *Journey to Zion: Voices from the Mormon Trail*. Salt Lake City: Deseret Book, 1997.

Merrill, Milton R. *Reed Smoot: Apostle in Politics*. Logan, Utah: Utah State University Press, 1990.

Middlemiss, Clare, comp. *Man May Know for Himself: Teachings of President David O. McKay*. Salt Lake City: Deseret Book, 1967.

Morrison, Alexander B. *The Dawning of a Brighter Day: The Church in Black Africa*. Salt Lake City: Deseret Book, 1990.

Newell, Linda King, and Valeen Tippetts Avery. *Mormon Enigma: Emma Hale Smith*. Urbana and Chicago: University of Illinois Press, 1994.

Parry, Jay A., and Larry E. Morris. *The Mormon Book of Lists*. Salt Lake City: Bookcraft, 1987.

Peterson, Janet, and LaRene Gaunt. *The Children's Friends: Primary Presidents and Their Lives of Service*. Salt Lake City: Deseret Book, 1996.

———. *Elect Ladies*. Salt Lake City: Deseret Book, 1990.

Pratt, Parley P. *Autobiography of Parley P. Pratt*. Ed. Parley P. Pratt Jr. Salt Lake City: Deseret Book, 1938, 1985.

Pusey, Merlo J. *Builders of the Kingdom: George A. Smith, John Henry Smith, George Albert Smith*. Provo, Utah: Brigham Young University Press, 1981.

Quinn, D. Michael. *J. Reuben Clark: The Church Years*. Provo, Utah: Brigham Young University Press, 1983.

Roberts. B. H. *A Comprehensive History of The Church of Jesus Christ of*

Latter-day Saints, Century One. 6 vols. Salt Lake City: The Church of Jesus Christ of Latter-day Saints, 1930.

———. *The Life of John Taylor, Third President of The Church of Jesus Christ of Latter-day Saints.* Salt Lake City: George Q. Cannon & Sons, 1892.

Rogers, Aurelia Spencer. *Life Sketches of Orson Spencer and Others, and History of Primary Work.* Salt Lake City: George Q. Cannon & Sons, 1898.

Romney, Thomas C. *The Life of Lorenzo Snow, Fifth President of The Church of Jesus Christ of Latter-day Saints.* Salt Lake City: Sugarhouse Press, 1955.

Smith, Henry A. *Matthew Cowley: Man of Faith.* Salt Lake City: Bookcraft, 1954.

Smith, Hyrum M., and Scott G. Kenney. *From Prophet to Son: Advice of Joseph F. Smith to His Missionary Sons.* Salt Lake City: Deseret Book, 1981.

Smith, Joseph. *History of The Church of Jesus Christ of Latter-day Saints.* Ed. B. H. Roberts, 7 vols. 2d ed. rev. Salt Lake City: Deseret Book, 1948.

Smith, Joseph Fielding. *Life of Joseph F. Smith.* Salt Lake City: Deseret Book, 1938.

Smith, Joseph Fielding Jr., and John J. Stewart. *The Life of Joseph Fielding Smith.* Salt Lake City: Deseret Book, 1972.

Smith, Lucy. *Biographical Sketches of Joseph Smith the Prophet, and His Progenitors for Many Generations.* Liverpool: S. W. Richards, 1853. In Vogel, vol. 1, 227–450.

Snow, Eliza R. *Biography and Family Record of Lorenzo Snow.* Salt Lake City: Deseret News Company, 1884.

Staker, Susan, ed. *Waiting for World's End: The Diaries of Wilford Woodruff.* Salt Lake City: Signature Books, 1993.

Tate, Lucile C. *Boyd K. Packer: A Watchman on the Tower.* Salt Lake City: Bookcraft, 1995.

Taylor, Samuel W. *The Last Pioneer: John Taylor, a Mormon Prophet*. Salt Lake City: Signature Books, 1999.

Terzian, James P. *The Many Worlds of Herbert Hoover*. New York: Julian Messner, 1966.

Vogel, Dan, ed. and comp. *Early Mormon Documents, Volume I*. Salt Lake City: Signature Books, 1996.

———. *Early Mormon Documents, Volume II*. Salt Lake City: Signature Books, 1998.

———. *Early Mormon Documents, Volume III*. Salt Lake City: Signature Books, 2000.

Wetterau, Bruce. *The New York Public Library Book of Chronologies*. New York: Prentice Hall Press, 1990.

INDEX

⎯

Aaronic Priesthood, restoration of, 128–29
Africa, 155–57, 158–62, 163–65
Anderson, May, 145–46
Armenia, 171
Arrington, Leonard J., 167
Articles of Faith, 188–89

Babbel, Frederick W., 20
Bateman, Merrill J., 161
Bennion, Adam S.: call as an apostle,
    106–7; letter from Hugh B. Brown to,
    106–7; death of, 108
Bennion, Minerva Young, 107
Bennion, Susan Marian Winters, 149
Benson, Ezra Taft: visit to Polish Saints,
    20–22; letter to Flora Amussen Benson,
    21–22; death of, 23; as President of the
    Church, 23; as Secretary of Agriculture,
    23; call as an apostle, 150; on pride,
    172–73
Benson, Flora Amussen: letter from Ezra
    Taft Benson to, 21–22; death of, 23
Bidamon, Lewis and Emma, 135
Boggs, Lilburn, 180, 186
Book of Abraham, 180
Book of Mormon: translation of, 73–74,
    80–81, 126–27; publication of, 74–76;
    coming forth of, 181–84
Booth, Delia Ina Winters, 149
Boulton, Curtis E., 38, 39
Boynton, John F., 9, 137
Brown, Hugh B.: marriage to Zina Card
    Brown, 24; death of, 25, 108; letter to
    Zina Card Brown, 25; love for Zina Card
    Brown, 25; as oil company manager and
    general counsel, 106; letter to Adam S.
    Bennion, 106–7; call as an apostle, 108;
    call as an Assistant to the Twelve, 108;
    on Reed Smoot, 195

Brown, Hugh Card, 25
Brown, Zina Card: marriage to Hugh B.
    Brown, 24, 107; death of, 25; letter from
    Hugh B. Brown to, 25
BYU Jerusalem Center for Near Eastern
    Studies, 167

Callis, Charles A.: as Southern States
    Mission president, 43, 45, 151; letter to
    Kathleen Callis Larsen, 43–45; death of
    twin sons, 45–46; call as an apostle, 46,
    152–53; letter from James E. Talmage to,
    151–52; organization of first stake in the
    South, 153; death of, 153–54
Callis, Charles Albert, 45–46
Callis, Grace Pack, 43, 151, 153–54
Callis, Nephi Quilliam, 45–46
Callis, Paul John, 200, 205
Camp of Israel, 131
Cannon, Edwin Q., 157, 160, 161
Cannon, Janath, 161
Card, Charles Ora, 24, 53
Card, Zina Young: response to Hugh B.
    Brown's request to marry daughter, 24;
    marriages and family of, 53;
    accomplishments of, 53–54; letter to
    Susa Young Gates, 54–55; death of, 55
Chase, John Paul, 203
Children's Friend, 146
Christiansen, ElRay L., 108
Clark, J. Reuben, Jr.: public service of, 197;
    political views of, 197–99; letter from
    Herbert Hoover to, 198; death of, 199;
    on use of the atomic bomb, 199
Clayton, Diantha Farr: death of, 13;
    marriage to William Clayton, 13; letter
    to William Clayton, 13–14; reunion
    with William Clayton, 14
Clayton, Moroni, 14–15